Will Allen Dromgoole

The Valley Path

Will Allen Dromgoole

The Valley Path

ISBN/EAN: 9783744743303

Printed in Europe, USA, Canada, Australia, Japan

Cover: Foto ©Andreas Hilbeck / pixelio.de

More available books at **www.hansebooks.com**

The Valley Path

By

Will Allen Dromgoole

Author of "The Heart of Old
Hickory," "The Farrier's
Dog and His Fellow,"
etc.

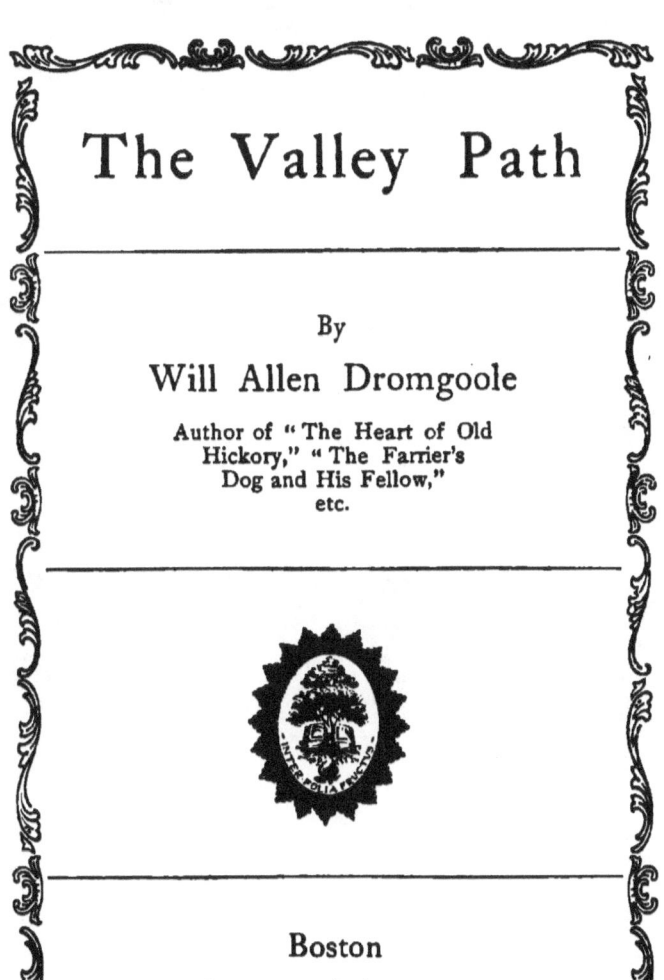

Boston
Estes and Lauriat
MDCCCXCVIII

To the two
who gave me life, and
made it worth the living: my father,

John Easter Dromgoole,

who was my guide and counsellor, my friend,
my comrade, and my critic, until God took him;
and my mother,

Rebecca Mildred Blanch,

whose faith and love have been my inspiration,
and who lingers in my life, a sweet and
gentle presence, for ever. Both of
whom, by God's good grace,
I humbly hope to
meet again.

THE love which desolated life, yet made
So dear its desolation; and the creeds
Which, one by one, snapped in my hold like reeds,
Beneath the weight of need upon them laid.

    .   .   .   .   .   .

Alas! 'tis not the creed that saves the man;
It is the man that justifies the creed;
And each must save his own soul as he can,
Since each is burthened with a different need.

           The Wanderer: ROBERT, LORD LYTTON.

The Valley Path

> THIS clay well mixed with marl and sand,
> Follows the motion of my hand:
> For some must follow and some command,
> Though all are made of clay.
> — "Kéramos."

Chapter I

AT the foot of the crags stood the doctor's cabin, a gray bird in a nest of green. Above it, the white mists ascending and descending about the heights of Sewanee; below, a brown thread in winter, in summer a strip of gay green, the pleasant valley of the Elk; through the valley — now lisping along its low banks, now cutting its course, a mountain torrent, through a jungle of cedar and ivy and laurel, the everlasting greens — the Elk itself, gurgling gaily down to meet the Tennessee; and through the valley, in and out among the greens, climbing the mountain farther back, the old brown footpath that used to pass the doctor's door. Making a turn or two, it also passed the door of the next house, a little white-washed cabin, set back in a clearing which Alicia Reams, the miller's granddaughter, used to call her "truck-patch." Singing among her pea-rows, summer days, her voice would come down to the doctor under his own vine and fig-tree, mixing and mingling strangely with his fancies.

The click-clack of the mill on Pelham Creek might be heard, too, as far as the doctor's, such days when toll was plenty and the wind not contrary.

It was only a step from the doctor's house to Alicia's, by way of the brown footpath, and he was a frequent visitor at the miller's. Yet were their lives far enough apart, for all the connecting path. For Jonathan Reams was a dusty old fellow in jeans, a homespun that was considered only the better for being unbleached. Of a pattern was the miller with his wife, familiarly known, as mountain mothers are, as "granny." Of a pattern the two so far as appearances went; no further; for granny was querulous and "fixed in her ways some." Any hour of the day, when she was not dozing over her pipe, either upon the hearth or under Alicia's honeysuckle vines, her voice might be heard scolding the miller, calling to Alicia to "shoo the chickens out of the gyarden," singing the praises of the herb-doctor or the psalms of the Methodists, as her mood might move her. Alicia's mother, however, had "been a schoolma'am once, befo' she died," and had taught her children, Al and "Lissy," something of books. She had been a dreamer, evidently, who had mistaken brawn for manhood, and so married Jed

Reams, the miller's son. The mother died, for grief of her mistake; the father, like other miller's sons, from natural causes. The boy Al inherited the mother's frail physique; to the girl fell her qualities of soul. Humble folks enough were they.

There was a silver doorplate on the doctor's door:

BARTHOLOMEW BORING, M. D.

Within, there were books, carpets, and servants: those marks of culture, and, they said, of the "eccentric." Such they were pleased to call him, those who had known him, before the valley knew him, for a friend. He might have walked the heights; that he found the valley paths more to his taste, the years in which he trod their humble ways bore evidence. That he had been ignorant of those unpretentious ways the first days of his coming, the silver plate bore evidence. When he did fall into line with all about him, the silver plate furnished so much of wonder and amusement that he let it be. And there it is to this good day:

BARTHOLOMEW BORING, M. D.

They had come for miles to look at it; come horseback and afoot, singly and in squads. They had wondered if M. D. might not be a warning, like "hands off," or "look out for pickpockets," or "don't tramp on the grass," until at last a shrewd young giant from across the mountain made out to read the riddle:

"It stands for *mad*," he declared. "'Bartholomew Borin', *Mad* Doctor.' That's what the sign says."

From that time he was placed, labelled like a vial of his own strychnine; *the mad doctor*.

He chuckled, enjoying the joke as keenly as its perpetrators. He even swore they were right: "Else why should a 'man forsake houses, and brethren, or wife'"— and there he stopped, as he always did, to sigh. Wife; that was the pivot upon which his fate had turned; swung from sun to shade, to rest at last under the stiller shadows of the wilderness.

The footpath way became familiar with his tread, and with his thoughts,

"If things inanimate catch heart-beats."

He was fond of its varied windings among the dusky glooms, and sunnier ways. The brown trail had been first opened by the cattle that went up daily to graze upon the long, lush plateau grasses, stopping by the way to touch their nozzles to the cooling waters of the Elk. Later, the opening in the brake became a footpath for the people on the mountain's side who came down Sabbath mornings to worship in the valley "meet'n-house" at Goshen, near unto Pelham Creek.

"Because," they said, "the Episcopers had tuk the mount'n bodaciously, callin' of it S'wany." And "Furthermore," they said, "Episcoper an' mount'neer won't mix worth mentionin'."

And so the mountain monarch had followed the example of his red brother and "moved on," leaving the plateau to the "Episcopers," who planted their flag, erected their homes, and worshipped their God under the beautiful groves of Sewanee. But to this good day, "Episcoper" and mountaineer refuse to mix, "worth mentionin'."

The doctor "mixed" with them as little as his rustic neighbours.

"They're out of my beat," he would declare, pointing along the footpath. "Too high," pointing up the mountain, "too *church*. I like this better."

He seldom followed the path further than the foot of the mountain, unless he had a patient up there, as was sometimes the case, among the very poor, the natives, living along the steep. He would walk to the spot where the path made a turn at Alicia's truck-patch, and stand leaning over the palings of Alicia's fence, talking with grandad Reams, the miller, about heaven, perhaps, until dismissed by granny from the doorstep, as "a doggone infidel."

Sometimes it was with Alicia that he talked; about the chickens, the eggs he wanted her to fetch over, or to ask if little Al was ailing. Sometimes he only walked there to look up at the heights, and at Sewanee, and to wonder concerning its creeds and dogmas. But he always called over the fence to Alicia, for some one thing or another.

"Just for the pure pleasure of hearing her laugh," he told himself; "it is like the gurgle of Elk River among the gray rocks at low-water time." He remembered the first time he ever walked there and saw the bright head among the corn rows, and heard the little gurgling laugh, and met the honest gray eyes with their untroubled deeps, and felt the force of her beautiful character, abloom like the sturdy mountain-laurel among the secluded ways of the wilderness. He remembered her hands, and the first strong clasp of her fingers, and the gentleness of their touch the first time he ever met her, in a cabin by the Pelham Road, with a dead babe lying across her knees, and those strong, gentle fingers feeling for its heart, that had fluttered like a wounded bird's and then—stopped. She had looked like a Madonna, with her motherly arms and sweet girl-face. In his fancy he had called her "the Madonna," that first time he saw her. And he had wondered then—but if he is going back to that "first time" when, yielding to a whim, or an inspiration, he had bidden the old walks farewell, sent his servants on to prepare a place where he might set his foot down free of creeds and memories and heartaches; and had sought the cabin in the wilds, cast his lot among the humble dwellers there, and had stumbled upon other creeds and memories and heartaches, why, we will turn the page and go with him, back to that *first time* when, among the Tennesseean vales, in a cabin in the wilderness, he encountered Alicia, the miller's granddaughter,— *his* Madonna.

Women know their fate the moment they know anything; with a change in the pattern of a dress their destinies are fairly one; with, perchance, this slight variety,— wife, spinster. But men stumble upon a strange destiny as they stumble upon one another; along the crowded walk, in the glare and glow of gaslight, in the ballroom, in the quiet woodland ways; after their rose-dreams have ended, it may be, along with youth and youthful fancies. Yet are the colours of the afterglow warmer, less blinding, than the sun's rays at meridian.

Chapter II

THE workmen had gone back to the city, and the house had been in all readiness for more than a week, when a trap set the doctor, and his terrier Zip, down at the gate of that which he was pleased to term his "mountain home."

Aunt Dilce had scrubbed and rubbed and made things "homeful" within doors, while her son Ephraim had performed a like service in stable and yard. Both servants, however, felt that it was so much good labour gone for naught: so much care put upon a cabin that was *only* a cabin when all was said and done. The only redeemable feature about the business was that it was all for the master, and was one of his whims, of which, they doubted not, he would soon tire.

True, there was the silver doorplate: to

be sure, that covered a multitude of evils. Aunt Dilce felt an honest town pride in that doorplate. The workmen whom the doctor had sent up to attend to things, and who had put the plate in place, were scarcely outside the gate before old Dilce was polishing the bit of silver "fit to kill." She kept it up every day until the doctor arrived. When the natives began to ride by and peep over the low fence at the little shining square, the old woman only polished the more vigorously. When they opened the gate, and, striding up the walk to the door, stood spelling out "the sign," her pride in it became such that she would certainly have rubbed it out of countenance but for the doctor's rush to the rescue.

It was the morning after his arrival, a morning in early spring. The laurel was in bloom along the river bluffs, and a quince-tree in the corner of the yard near the fence gave promise of bursting buds.

The doctor rose early,—"an indication

of old age," he told himself,—and called for his coffee.

"Throw open the windows," he said to Ephraim, "then hand me my purple dressing-gown, and tell your mother I want my coffee. I want it hot,—as hot as—"

"Here 'tis, marster; en yo' bre'kfus' 'll be raidy in a minute." The old woman had appeared most opportunely: the doctor was about to let slip his one pet profanity.

He laughed softly as he slipped into his purple robings and his easy chair, and, leaning his big gray head back against the velvet rest, he prepared to enjoy the coffee, which old Dilce was arranging on the stand at his right hand.

There was a click of the little gate latch; the "big gray" was lifted; through the open window came the fresh, sweet river-breath, and the far-away odour of new mould where some industrious plowman was overturning the sod, further down the valley. And through the window the twinkling blue eyes saw a long, lank figure, followed by another and another, amble up to his doorstep, stop a moment, and move on, making room for the next, like a procession at a public funeral stopping to look at the corpse in state. Full twenty passed in at the gate and out again. The master turned to Dilce:

"What the hell are they doing?" he demanded; and then came old Dilce's turn at chuckling.

"Hit's de do' fixin's, marster," she declared. "Dem do' fixin's am too fine fur dese parts; en dey ain' showin' ob you de proper respec', accordin' ter my suppression. Yistiddy one o' de stroppinist ones ob dem all nicknamed ob you 'de Mad Doctor.' He say dat what de sign mean; M. D. — 'Dat mean Mad Doctor,' he say."

The gray head went back upon the velvet chair-rest, and a laugh echoed among the rafters and sills and beams of the gray cabin, such as they had not heard since rescued from the owl, the bat, and the gopher, to make room for the medicine boxes and books of the "mad doctor."

"It is enough to made them think me a lunatic," he told himself, as all day the passers-by stopped to wonder at the reckless waste of silver. "And when they discover that I am not here to practise, but merely to nurse a whim and a disposition to cynicism and catarrh, they will think me madder still,—rip, ranting mad. '*The other side*' thought the same, because I refused to put the plate on a door in the city. Well, well; we'll see, we'll see. Maybe there will be no call for declining to practise," he laughed, softly, "among my new neighbours. At all events, I need not refuse until the arrival of my first patient."

Sure enough, as he had half expected, they set him in the balance at once. "Against herbs and conjure and hornets," he said, whenever he told the joke, as he certainly did tell it, to any of his former friends who hunted him up now and then by a visit to his "shanty," or sent him an invitation to meet them at Sewanee, the Episcopal seat of learning.

They set him in the balance the very first day of his arrival. He was strolling about the yard among the flower beds Ephraim was laying off, enjoying his modest possessions in his own cranky old way, bareheaded, the sun making a sparkle of his wavy hair that touched the purple velvet collar of his robe, working a pleasant contrast even in the eyes of the young giant riding along the footpath towards the gate.

To a mind more familiar with the æsthetic might have occurred some pretty imagery, some blend of colour, gray and purple, like the mists that covered the mountain-top. But the visitor was a stranger to æsthetics. He saw the gray head and the purple gown, the kindly, old-young face, with its laughing eyes half hidden under the bushy brows. If he made any comparison, nobody knew it. There were curiosity, eagerness, business, in the man's whole appearance; in the very trot of the yellow mule upon whose bare back he sat astride, his own bare feet almost touching the ground on either side.

At the visitor's "Halloo," the doctor looked up from the mignonette bed; something told him this was the arrival of his first patient. The two regarded each other steadily. What the doctor saw was a slender-built young fellow, with clean, sharply defined features, blue eyes that were wells of mirth, a chin which meant defiance, a brow browned by the valley sun, and, pushed back with careless, unconscious grace, an old slouch hat, the inevitable adornment of his class. A mass of soft, clinging curls gave a girlish something to the defiant face. The full, beardless lips were ready to break into smiles, despite the scowl with which their owner was regarding this newcomer to the valley.

In this newcomer the visitor saw a young-old face; the eyes and smile of youth, the lines and snow of age on brow and temple. Beyond the physician the mountaineer saw the silver doorplate and its flaunting M. D., and seeing, took courage.

"Air you the town doctor?" he demanded, flecking a cockle-bur from the yellow mule's comb with the tip of a willow withe, which served him as a riding-whip.

"Yes," said the doctor, "I am; and a mighty good one at that."

The visitor lifted his big, bare foot and planted it upon the topmost rail of the gray worm fence, almost under the very nose of the Æsculapius, and, pointing with the willow switch to his great toe, swollen and red and distorted, demanded:

"What ails *hit*?"

The professor of three diplomas put on his spectacles: the toe was three times its ordinary size; the flesh was raw-looking and ugly; he touched it gingerly with his practised fingers.

"A bad toe," he declared, in his slow, professional voice. Ephraim, the bow-legged boy of all work, had sauntered up, dragging his hoe after him; Aunt Dilce was listening, arms akimbo, from the corner of the house.

"That, sir," the physician explained, "is what we doctors call a pretty bad case of erysipelas."

The mountaineer reined in the yellow mule. "Erysip'lis *hell!*" he replied. "A hornet stung it."

The mule went down the road to Pelham in a cloud of yellow dust. Old Dilce ambled back to the kitchen with her cotton apron stuffed into her mouth. Ephraim stumbled back to his mignonette bed. The doctor suddenly turned upon him: "You Ephraim?"

"Yes, sah!"

Ah! he *was* showing his ivories.

"If you ever tell that to a living soul, sir, I'll break every bone in your body; do you hear, sir?"

He could, however, hear Aunt Dilce chuckling over the cake she was about to slap upon the hoe, that had become too hot while she had been enjoying the call of the master's first patient.

Yet, that first patient proved another pivot upon which life made a turn; such is the unsuspected magnitude of trifles. It was the real beginning of his life in the little cove tucked away among the spurs of the Cumberlands, where he had elected to pass his summers,—not his life. That he would have other patients he never once considered; no more did he moralise upon "the opportunities of doing good," which had become too much of a phrase to hold real earnest meaning. He had given up moralising long ago; while as for *opportunities*, he rather thought of them as something either self-creative or thrust upon one. That they would come he took for granted, though he refused to seek them. When, at last, one tapped at his door, he did not recognise it at all, hearing in its voice only the cry of suffering humanity; he merely buttoned on his coat and went to meet it, that was all.

Chapter III

DURING the next week the physician from the city heard more than once how "Joe Bowen had gotten ahead o' the mad doctor." He had been questioned about it when he went over to the little country town of Moffat, and had even told the joke of his own accord, laughing at it as heartily as the rest. It proved an introduction for him, at all events, and went to verify the old saying that "a bad reputation is better than none." The people roundabout heard of him as a physician, and one afternoon, about ten days after Joe had made his call, the doctor had a second.

A man from up the valley, in passing, left word of "a fambly o' children down with scyarlet fever, in a house on the Pelham road." He "reckined they'd take it mighty kind if the mad doctor'd step over an' see what he could do for 'em."

Being a three-mile "step," he ordered his horse; and as a *family* had been attacked with the disease, he carried his medicine-case along.

It was his first ride down the Pelham road, and, notwithstanding there were suffering children at the end of his journey, he rode slowly. The young spring was abroad; the woods were a mass of quivering new greens; the trees alive with birds; where he crossed Pelham Creek the water rose with a sibilant gurgle to the bay mare's belly. The birds made merry over their nests in the heart of the laurel-brake; in the tops of the red oak-trees a little mountain oriole was calling, — calling in his half-merry, half-melancholy song, the first note of which is a whistle, the second an inquiry, the third a regret, and the fourth an unmistakable sigh, — a trill of music and a wail of melancholy. The good green grass crowded the roadside; the wild honeysuckle nodded to him from the deeper hollows of the wood; the very winds that fanned his cheek were gentle, kind, sympathetic. He scarcely saw, he only felt, the glad new restfulness of living.

"It was a wise move," he murmured, "a very wise move. I am glad I came to the wilderness." He rode on for a moment in silence, the mare's feet scarcely audible in the light green sward of the almost untravelled valley road. Suddenly he lifted his head and looked about him, snuffing the keen, spring-scented air.

"What a place to die in!" he exclaimed; "to grow old and die in. Up, now! we are loitering in this Sleepy Hollow."

He touched the mare's neck with the bridle-rein lightly, and ere long the restful woods, with their seduction of sound and colour, lay behind him.

It was noon when he reached the house, one of the ordinary two-room log cabins of the neighbourhood, having a shed in the rear, and an open passage between the living-rooms.

An old woman, tall and gaunt and cadaverous-looking, occupied the little homemade bench that adorned the passage; before her stood a large jar, a crock, surmounted by a wooden top; the crock was doing duty as churn; the woman was industriously plying the dasher. She rose, when the doctor drove up, and called to him to "turn his nag in the yard, else it would be worrit ter death by a loose mule o' Joe Bowenses that was rampantin' the country."

He obeyed instructions, and in a moment more stood in the passage, inquiring after the sick.

"They're right in thar," said the woman, "if you're the doctor man."

"Are they yours?"

"Naw, sir, they ain't mine, an' I'm glad of it, bein' as they're all three 'bout ter die. One of 'em's in an' about dead, I reckin. I ain't got but one, an' he's a man growed. Though I ain't tellin' of you, doctor, that I never had no more. I've done my part, I reckin; I've got 'leven dead ones. I failed ter raise 'em; the measles an' the whoopin'-cough an' the fever set in an' they all went,—all but Jim. Jim he tuk the jaundice once't, but he got over it. I'm mighty glad ter meet you, Doctor Borin'."

"Thank you, madam," replied the physician, with such honest simplicity and hearty sincerity that the woman's sallow face beamed the pleasure the words gave her. It was only a simple greeting from a gentle heart; but because of it the mad doctor had one friend more upon the list of those who loved him.

"Do you live here?" he asked.

"Naw, sir; I live in the first house on the road ter S'wany, back o' yo' place. My name's Tucker; Mis' Tucker. You can go in now an' see the child'en, Doctor Borin', if you please ter; I come over ter try an' help a bit, an' I'll jist churn this milk an' give Lissy a swaller o' fresh buttermilk. Pears like she can't be persuaded ter take time to eat nothin'."

He glanced carelessly at the low-ceiled room, the two beds occupying two corners, the small trundle-bed drawn into the centre of the room, and the little square window which did duty in the way of light and ventilation, the batten shutter thrown wide open. A boy of ten years lay tossing upon the trundle-bed, flushed and fretting with fever. Upon another bed, listless, and pale as marble, a young girl was lying. Hers was a complicated case, and might prove a hopeless one. The great, hollow eyes were turned to the door, watching the doctor; a low, panting moan issued continually from the thin, bloodless lips.

He took it all in at a glance; the poverty, the crowded, close air, the ignorance of disease, and the suffering occasioned thereby. But that which appealed to him above all things was the figure of a young girl seated beside an empty cradle, with a little baby upon her knees, her hand lying lightly upon its breast. At first he had seen in the uncertain light only a coil of bright hair, of that peculiar shade that is neither gold nor auburn; it was more like a dab of warm sunshine in the gloom of the place. As his eye became accustomed to the gloom, the outline of the face grew broader, and he saw where womanly tenderness and sweetness blended into a Madonna-like perfection of beauty. She wore a dress of some dark stuff, opened at the throat, and with the sleeves pushed back in clumsy little rolls above the dimpled elbows, plump and shapely. Her face was bent over the child upon her lap, and her slender, strong fingers were feeling under the bosom of the little white gown for the baby's heart.

She lifted her head when the physician bent over her to look into the small, smiling face against her knee. Even then he noticed that the large gray eyes lifted to his were tearless, the slender fingers were firm and without a tremor; if she felt an emotion she held it magnificently in control.

"Go to the others," she said, in a quietly impressive tone. "Go to the others; it ain't no use to waste time here. I felt its heart stop beatin' when I heard your step in the passage. I ain't been able to find it any more."

Not even when she began to smooth the lids down over the staring baby's eyes, did the slender fingers falter.

"Its ma is down in the orchard with its pa," she continued, when the physician questioned her concerning the parents. "They went out to keep from seein' it die. But it died mighty easy; there was nothing to run from as I can see,—jest a little baby going to sleep."

The slender fingers went on smoothing the dead eyes; there was a caressing something about the manner in which they moved, that robbed their task of horror. The physician regarded her steadily a moment.

"Are you one of the family?" he asked. "Do you belong here?"

"No, sir," she replied, in her soft, musical drawl. "I live in the house nearest yours; I'm Alicia Reams, the miller's granddaughter. They call me 'Lissy' for short. I'm just here to help some; so if you want anything I can get it for you. So can Mrs. Tucker, if you'll speak to her outside the door there."

"Well," said the physician, "I 'want' a good deal. First thing, I want that churn stopped, or carried out of reach of the ears of this nervous girl here. Then I want to separate living and dead in this house, or we shall have more dead in a little while. Isn't there another room across the passage?"

"Yes, sir. If you'll call Mrs. Tucker to take the baby I'll help you with the others."

She placed the dead child in the arms of the older woman, directed her where to find its "things," and sent her into the shed-room to make the tiny body ready for burial. Then she gave a little tuck in her sleeves, and, turning to the physician, said, in a whisper:

"I'm goin' to run down in the orchard and send the baby's pa to Cowan after a coffin and things; I'll come right back in a minute. Try and do somethin' for Cora; she's suffered lots, Cora has."

She flitted away like a dash of lost sunshine, leaving the real gloom of death in the room. Yet her presence lingered; the low, sweet cadence of her voice still sounded in the doctor's ears; the bright face, with its great gray eyes, — "shadow pools," he called them, — was still before him. What a face it was: neither girl's nor woman's, yet — lacking. There were fire, warmth, feeling; a native refinement marked her handling of even the ordinary coarser duties which devolved upon her;

there was gentleness in every motion of the body. The touch of her fingers was magnetic: her hand had brushed his when he examined the baby upon her knees, and it had thrilled him as he had not been thrilled in years. How strong her presence, outlined against the weakness about her. Already he had begun to speculate concerning her; surely the girl had possibilities, — a future something beyond the listless lives about her, — ran his thought. She was at his side again while he was trying to solve the riddle of her.

"Now, Doctor Borin'," she said, "I'm ready to help you do something for these. I'm ready to take hold, and you needn't mind telling me; I'm used to doin' for the sick. There's been a good deal o' sickness in this valley, and I've learned to help some, bein' as help was scarce."

Together they worked; he directing, and lending a hand when one was needed, as it often was. In a little while the sick had been removed into the room across the passage, and made comfortable in the fresh, sweet beds for which the humblest of the region are known. The boy was soon fast asleep under the doctor's ministrations. The case of Cora, the young girl, was not so easily managed. Fever had started again, and the scene through which she had just passed, the grief-stricken mother, the dead baby, the restless fretfulness of her brother, had so excited the patient that the physician found it difficult to calm her. He remained until dusk, and returned again after supper, remaining until midnight, gently soothing his patient, until, with the aid of his skill and a subtle something in his presence, she fell into a deep slumber. At midnight he left Alicia in charge.

"Allow no one to enter the room," he said to her as they stood together for a moment in the passage, where a feeble old lantern was doing its best, with the assistance of the moon, in the matter of lighting the way for the neighbours who dropped in at all hours of the night to "sit up with the corpse" in the family room. "Nobody must go in there except you or Mrs. Tucker; she has the gift of discretion as well as yourself. Above all things, keep from the sick children what is going on in the next room. I will return at eight o'clock to-morrow; can you hold out so long?"

He could almost see the laugh in her gray eyes, lifted to his, by the sickly light of the lantern.

"I'm good for a week yet, Doctor Borin'," she said. "Hold out! you don't know Lissy Reams."

"I *shall* know her," he replied, "if she is to set herself up as my rival, or my partner, in practice here."

He heard her low, gurgling laugh, instantly checked as she remembered the presence in the cabin. "We're neighbours," she said; "I have got a little truck-patch where I raise things to sell at

S'wanee. I'll fetch you over a mess of beans soon; see if I don't."

"And all the fresh eggs you can spare," said the doctor. "I want to engage them now, for *years, — as long as I live.*"

"Heish," she said, softly, "don't make me laugh. It ain't kind, at a time like this. Besides, I might die long befo' you, — who knows?"

"You? Look at those arms, will you? Then go look in the glass, and see the blood come and go in your cheeks. Moreover, old Dilce, my housekeeper, tells me that you go up the mountain every morning by sunup, and in a *canter*. In a canter,—think of it! I couldn't walk up in a day. And you talk of dying before me. Tut! Let me hear you laugh again."

But the laugh did not come; gazing full into his eyes, she had found there nothing, notwithstanding the lightness of his tone, to encourage mirth. In the lantern's light the doctor saw an unmistakable shadow, faint, vague, and fleeting, hover for an instant in her eyes.

"I ain't always so lively," she said, slowly, "nor so reasonable, neither, I reckon. Sometimes I have the blues awful, and then I'm just good for nothin'. I ain't any help to anybody when I get the blues. And most of the time it's just about nothin' I have 'em. Ain't I an awful goose?"

As if the confession were precisely that which he had expected, he said, in a vague, dreamful tone, "I know,—yes, I understand."

"Doctor Borin'?" The eager surprise in her voice quite startled him.

"Why, you see," he said in explanation, "we doctors possess certain secret entrances to the soul, not permitted others. We understand character as well as body. Now you are what we in our profession would call ethereal,—that is, pertaining to the spirit. You are a dreamer."

She laughed softly, under her breath,

lest the gay sound should reach the troubled ear of the bereaved, and jar unpleasantly.

"I'm a peddler of truck," she replied. "I sell vegetables to the college boardin'-house at S'wanee. In the winter I sell butter and eggs and dried beans to the same house. That's my life pretty much, and that's the kind of dreamer I am. Though I ain't sayin' but I'd like—"

"There," said he, "I told you so. Your garden rows are full of your dreams, dropped in with your seed. And your egg basket wouldn't begin to hold the fancies that fill your heart while you trip up the mountain to Sewanee."

He left her standing in the passage, her bare arms folded upon her breast and gleaming like silver in the mingled light of moon and lantern. The picture of her stayed with him while he rode home in the soundless midnight; the fair young face with that dainty mingling of colour which belongs alone to first sweet youth;

the coy blending of girl and woman; the graceful, well-fulled body; and the soul lurking in the gray deeps of eyes which, once seeing, would for ever refuse the darkness of life's ways. Out of place, — as much out of place in that wilderness cabin as his silver doorplate on the hut at the foot of the mountain.

There was a tragedy in her life; the bare fact of her being was a tragedy, and could round to no other end than the tragic. Some souls are born to it; and whether they live quietly, unknown, and die tamely in their beds, unmourned, or whether their lives, like candles, are snuffed out at their best brightness, amid the lamentations of the multitude, matters nothing and alters nothing. The tragedy has been enacted; the soul has suffered, and has fulfilled that whereunto it was born.

Suddenly he gave the lines a quick, impatient jerk. " Bah ! " he exclaimed; then in a softer tone : " I am bewildered by a dash of yellow hair, and a dabble of pink and white cheeks. I am an old fool. The girl will marry some strapping mountaineer, rear a houseful of tow-headed children, wash, scrub, bake, and be happy, after the manner of her kind. But I believe — " The words were lost in a gurgle of water, — PelhamCreek among its gray rocks, winding down to meet him at the ford.

"Who knows? who knows?" Her words came back to him in the lisping flow as the mare's feet touched the moon-flecked flood. "I might die long before you, — who knows?"

"Who knows?" he mused; "who knows anything? And how little any of us know, for that matter. Yet *I* know the miller's grandchild, with half a showing, would not live the prosaic life of the mountaineer, despite the strong brown arms and the thriving 'truck-patch.'"

What a contrast she presented to the women he had known; what a contrast to *her*, that *one woman*, who stood out in his thoughts like a ghost in the midday,—a ghost that is not seen, but felt, and is cold, chilling the soul of warm life.

Then he thought of his friends at home, his former *confrères* and companions. What would they think of the extent to which his "crankiness" had carried him? — ministering in hovels at midnight, without so much as the mean motive of a few dollars by way of recompense.

"They may think as they choose," was his thought. "Most men, *all* men, I believe, have their cranks,—their 'ideal life' they call it. The only difference with us is that I am fool enough to indulge mine. I claim the right to live my own life,—to spoil it myself, rather than permit others to spoil it for me; since I spoil it at least in the faith that I am doing my best for it. And after all, life is a solitary thing, and must be lived alone. They who pass upon it and advise about it, can do no more; for life in the abstract, like death, knows no duality. Now this girl — but enough; I am an old fool."

Yet the picture of her stayed with him; and when at last he fell asleep in his own bed, drawn as he always had it, where the moonlight from the small old-fashioned window fell athwart his pillow, he still saw her, in a dream, sitting beside an empty cradle, with a little waxen baby on her knees.

Chapter IV

DOCTOR BORING had an early breakfast the next morning, and immediately after ordered his horse.

"They are as like as not to lay the corpse out on the bed with one of my patients," he said, in reply to Aunt Dilce's complaining. "Moreover, I left the little Reams woman there,"—it never occurred to him to call Alicia, as his mind had received its first impression of her, a girl,—"and she must be all used up by this time. One of those children is going to have a fight for life, and if I am to get in any work it must be at the start; there is scant need of a physician at the finish. I am going to send Alicia Reams over here, Aunt Dilce; and I want you to have a good hot breakfast for her, and make her take the time to eat it. Be good to her, black mammy; when she gets here, look after her; make her rest awhile. Then do you send the horse back to me."

He found Alicia as busy as though she had not lost a wink of sleep in a month. She was bending over a saucepan in the shed-room, mixing a meal poultice for Cora, who had complained of "a mis'ry in the side."

Doctor Boring went from room to room with the freedom to which they were too well accustomed to consider it presuming, until he found Alicia in the shed-room.

"I will attend to that," he said, indicating the poultice; "do you get on your bonnet and mount my horse,— can you ride?"

She nodded, smiling. "I've always lived nigh enough to the mount'n to be called a mount'n girl," she said; "an' mount'n girls can ride anything, from broomstick to steer. Is somebody else sick, an' you want me to go there, to help nurse 'em?"

"Hell!" he murmured. "Go there? *No!* I want you to mount that horse and get away from sick folks. Get away like you were getting away from Indians, measles, small-pox, yellow jackets. Do you understand?"

She set the saucepan upon the hearth and crammed her apron into her mouth.

"Great I am!" she exclaimed, when the disposition to laugh outright had been overcome. "I have *heard* you were wicked."

"You haven't heard the half," he replied. "Here! throw that mash in the pig-pen; I have a mustard plaster for the pain in the side. The children are both better. I am glad of that. I've got to prove to these people that I'm a doctor, even if I don't know a hornet's sting when it is thrust under my nose."

A flash of the gray eyes, a dimpling of the cheek, and a twitching of the red lips told him that she knew the story, though she said, with proper demureness, "Did somebody allow you didn't know the difference?"

"Oh, I didn't," he admitted, with open candour. "I was completely sold. But if I can help these little children back to health I am willing to take my chances with you people. Now, Lissy, you must do as I say. Aunt Dilce is holding your breakfast back until you come. You ride on to my house, take a good rest, a good breakfast, and then go home and go to bed."

"I ain't tired," she replied, "and I ought to stay here and help about buryin' of the baby."

"Burying be hanged!" he replied. "Unless you do as I tell you I shall go back and eat the breakfast myself, and leave the sick to go as the baby went. Do you understand? If you value your friends here, and my reputation as a physician, you must do as I command."

"Oh, these ain't my friends," she replied. "I never was here before."

"What? what are you doing here, then?"

"Helpin'," she replied. "I always help. That's all I *can* do; I'm an awful sinner — worse than you, I reckin. You'll hear all about it. But I can't help it; I'm bound to act accordin' to my light, and I haven't seen the way to the mourners' bench *yet*. And Brother Barry — he's the circuit-rider — he says I'm bound for hell and torment, and that I'm one o' the stiff-necked and hard of heart. Did you notice I didn't even cry when the baby died in my lap? I couldn't; all the rest cried. But me — I couldn't see what there was to sorrow about in a little baby jist slippin' from this world o' trouble up to God. It was all mighty sweet and happy to me. I was sort of glad to see it go; I knew it would never be worried with doubts, like me, nor be hindered none by lack o' light and grace. Doctor Borin', I hear Cora cryin' with the mis'ry in her side; won't you go in and put the mustard to it? An' I'll run 'long and get the breakfast you saved. It was mighty good of you. I'll sure enjoy it, I know I will. An' I'll surely fetch the mess o' beans by an' by, and fresh eggs enough for your many a breakfast. If," she added, roguishly, "you don't die of old age befo' the hens can get on their nestes."

When she had gone, although he gave his full attention to the sick, she was not once absent from his thoughts. If she had puzzled him the night before, the piquant beauty of her face only charmed and bewitched him the more in the good glow of the daylight. He had felt a great curiosity in seeing it again; without giving form to the doubt, he had somehow felt vaguely that something was lacking to the face's full perfection. She was not slow or dull, after the manner of the mountain maidens, owing perhaps to the influence and teachings of her valley mother. There was nothing stupid, none of the heavy country girl about her. Yet, when the large eyes looked full into his, he saw the wavering, weaker lights under the strong purplish gray; and when she had gone he whispered to his own inquiring heart: "A nature to be moulded; an impressionist, with a tendency towards the morbid."

It was noon when he left the house of mourning. The little baby had been laid to sleep in a neighbouring burying-ground, and the sick were doing reasonably well. He had found a good deal to contend with in the matter of the infant's burial. In the tall, gaunt minister who had arrived in time to conduct the services, and in the stupid persistence with which he insisted upon the performance of the duty upon which he had come, Doctor Boring recognised "Brother Barry," the Methodist circuit-rider. A funeral was expected, was customary; Brother Barry was not to be set aside by the ravings of an infidel. But when the infidel took the father of the dead babe aside, and swore in large round English that the singing and confusion would endanger the life of Cora, Brother Barry, for once in his life, was forced to the wall. So the men tiptoed into the passage, lifted the small pine coffin in their hands, and the rest followed noiselessly to the little grave that had been prepared in the valley shade, within reach of the lisping music of Elk River.

"The child will sleep as well without their howling," said the doctor, as the bay mare trotted along the valley road in the direction of home. "It will sleep as well, and wake as surely, — *if* they wake, those silent sleepers."

His thought took a sudden melancholy turn. He let the lines fall upon the bay's neck, and she fell into the ordinary jog-trot of animals less daintily sired than this glossy bay Morgan. She even stopped to seize a mouthful of the new greens crowding the roadside, without rebuke from the dreaming rider.

Suddenly he roused, and took up the lines sharply; his ear had caught a note of discord in the noontime harmony. He listened; a twinkle came into his eyes, and a smile parted for a moment his lips. He had almost reached the turn of the road where his cabin would stand revealed. Already he could see the low worm fence, which he meant to replace with a pretty paling by and by, and a raw-boned, flea-bitten mare that was cropping the new buds of his favourite quince-tree, to which she had been "hitched" by a bridle-rein twisted among the low-drooping branches that overhung the fence upon the outside. He had a caller. He recognised the flea-bitten mare; he had seen it at the baby's burial when Brother Barry rode up. He also recognised the voice of Aunt Dilce "laying the law down" to bow-legged Ephraim:

"You Efum? Git up from dar en

he'p dribe de peeg out'n de yard, fo' hit root all de marster's flowers up, an' hit dat peeg dar in de haid dis minute. Quit makin' all dat fuss ter let folks know dey done lef' de gate op'n, en tu'n all de peegs in de country in de yard. Sooey dar! Haid 'im off'n dat vi-let baid, nigger. Dar! dar he goes! knock 'im in de haid! Skeer 'im out'n dem chulups! en min' yo' own bus'ness! 'Tain' none yo' bus'ness ter let folks know dey done lef' de gate op'n, same lack dey ain' got no sense, en no raisin' nohow. Dar! hit dat peeg! Don't let 'im inter dat minuet baid, I tell yer. Call 'im off! Peeg? Peeg? Sooey dar, sooey! Call 'im! haid 'im dar fo' I knock you down wid dis here rock, en make you mo' bow-laigged en what you is a'raidy. Hit 'im! sooey dar! Whi' folks know niggers ain' got nuffin ter do 'cept ter run de hogs out. Dat's what de good Lord made dey-all fur; jes' ter 'commerdate po' white trash. Look at dat peeg! sooey! haid 'im dar! haid 'im! Now you got him! haid 'im off todes de gate. Dar! easy now — haid 'im in — Dat fool nigger done let dat horg slip froo his laigs."

The doctor heard every word; so too had the guest within doors, as Aunt Dilce meant he should. He saw the old woman's chase after the interloper, and recognised the jeopardy of his pets, the flower beds. Yet he smiled as he dismounted and tossed his bridle to Ephraim. The little gate still swung wide open upon its hinges, just as the visitor had left it; a pair of yellow, weather-beaten saddle-bags lay upon his doorstep, and Zip, his little black terrier, was industriously seeking an investigation of their contents.

It was the first call the circuit-rider had made at the cabin. The doctor chuckled.

"Liked my looks, I suppose," was his reflection, "or else he saw my chicken-coop; — these Methodists!"

Old Dilce, none the cleaner for her race

with the hog, hobbled forward to say, in the half-complaining tone familiar to her race:

"De preacher ob de gospil am in de house, marster; en he look lack he toler'ble hongry fur his dinner."

The doctor laughed softly, rescuing the saddle-bags, thereby bringing upon himself an onslaught from the terrier.

"Well, then," said he, "do you be sure you fix him up a good one."

"Who, me?"

"Yes, you. And tell Ephraim to take the mare to the barn."

The old woman's face wore a knowing look.

"He say he ain't got but jes' a minute ter set. He say he got ter be about his Marster's business."

"Yes," said the doctor, "I have heard something like that before. You had better get the dinner ready; chicken pie and apple dumplings."

Still she didn't move; evidently there

was news yet. He waited a moment for its coming:

"Dat little gal f'm down yon'er e't toler'ble hearty dis mawnin'."

"Who? what? Oh, Lissy. Did she? Well, I'm glad of that. She's a good girl. You must be good to Lissy."

"I sho am," was the hearty reply. "She mighty p'lite, en thankful. Dat little gal hab good raisin', sho's *you* bawn."

"Oh, get out with you," laughed the doctor, "the girl knows no more of courtesies than Zip here. Never been beyond the mountain in her life."

"Den she am a bawn lady," declared old Dilce, nothing daunted. "She ain' no po' white trash."

"See here now, Aunt Dilce, what did the girl give you? Oh, you needn't protest, I know well enough she bought you."

"'Fo' God, marster, she ain' gimme a bressed thing. She say she gwine fetch me some terbacky out'n o' her grandpa's patch bimeby, dat's all. En she say she wish ter de goodness you ud come over dar en see her grandpa; he's plumb peart en healthy en *dat* fond o' comfy! En she e't her bre'kfus toler'ble healfy; she sho did."

"Aunt Dilce," said the physician, "my tobacco box is on the mantel; help yourself, you sly old rogue. Now go and get the dinner for the preacher. I am going in to invite him to remain to it."

"You won't have ter baig, I'll be boun'," was the parting shot as she went back to her kitchen.

The doctor opened the door and went in. As he entered his cosy little study, a stalwart, robust figure, clad in a rusty black suit of clothes and carrying a worn silk hat in his hand, rose to meet him. The face wore a woebegone, lugubrious expression, as if the sins of the world had been too many for the broad, bent shoulders. A mass of long, sandy, unkempt hair lay upon the sleek collar of the ecclesiastic coat. He was a typical backwoods circuit-rider of the old time, when zeal was supposed to do duty for education; the air of conscious rectitude, of superior knowledge, and a friendly familiarity with the Holy of Holies that was vouchsafed to but few, stamped his calling beyond a shadow of doubting. He extended his hand to meet the physician's:

"I come in the name of the Master," said he.

"Well, you found the door open, at all events," replied the doctor. "I tarried awhile with the sick down the valley. Resume your seat, sir."

"Death and disease walk the earth," chanted the divine, in solemn measures. "Sorrow an' desolation walk hand in hand. One sows an' another reaps, and no man knoweth what a day may bring forth. My brother, I am come in the name of the Master. I come not to call the righteous but sinners to repentance. I have come to beg you to repent — to warn you, and to teach you."

"Wait until after dinner," said the doctor. "I'm a terrible old fool, I reckon, but I like to take my lesson on a full stomach. Sit down there, Brother Barry. I am going to fill a pipe for you, and introduce you to my dog Zip; then I am going to give you a good dinner, another pipe, and a peep at the prettiest colt in this valley. Then I am going to send you up those stairs into my guest-chamber, 'the upper room' where you are to have a bath, a nap, and remain as long as you choose. Heavens! don't object, man; doesn't your Methodist nose tell you there is chicken in the pot? Chicken pie; and here is Aunt Dilce come to tell us it is on the table. Come out; we will talk religion some other time."

Brother Barry, however, seemed disposed to argument.

"My Master's business,"—he protested, though decidedly more feebly than at first,—"I must be about it; I cannot tarry."

"Why," laughed the doctor, "I thought

you were sent here to seek a lost sheep. I tell you, sir, you've run against the toughest old ram that ever tried to butt its own brains out. You may spend a week on me if you are so inclined, but you are not commanded to starve meanwhile; on the other hand, you are told not to muzzle the ox that treadeth out the corn. Come out to your fodder."

The invitation was too hearty for resistance. The Methodist placed his tall hat on the table and followed the doctor out to dinner. It was the first of many they were to take together, these two whose lives were to cross, but not, in the finer sense, to touch; these two, the one broad and warm with the sunshine of all charity, the other narrow and ignorant and immovable, making religion a dark and unreal thing, and demanding of its advocates a life of perpetual gloom in a path beset by dangers, curses, terrors; these two, the one with his eye fixed ever upon the sun, the other a groveller among the glooms, believing always in the depravity of humanity and always bearing the burden of its rescue.

The Methodist made himself at home from the moment he entered the doctor's door. He was made as welcome as any might desire; only upon matters of religion the physician refused to talk. But Brother Barry was a man of infinite resources, and failing to take the doctor by one means he had recourse to others. That he would be converted at the last the circuit-rider held no shadow of doubt.

The first night of his arrival, when the physician had been sleeping for hours he was awakened by a tremendous thumping upon the floor of the chamber overhead.

He sprang from his bed with a start, and ran to the door of the little old-fashioned stairway that went up from his own bedroom. His thought was that Brother Barry was again "surrounding the throne," — an exercise that had kept him awake for more than an hour during the earlier night. But this was more serious; Brother Barry was calling for a light.

"Fetch a light, brother; fetch a light quick, and pencil and paper; I have got a thought."

The doctor's gray head was thrust into the doorway.

"Oh, you go to sleep, Brother Barry," said he, "and trust the Lord for another." And, closing the door, the old infidel went chuckling back to bed.

They were odd companions, these two; yet each was interesting to the other. The preacher regarded the doctor with a kind of pious pity, while the physician's feeling for him would have partaken largely of contempt, but that his good heart recognised the fact that the Methodist was honest even in his ignorance. After three days Brother Barry threw his saddle-bags across the back of the flea-bitten mare and took his departure. In that three days' time he had vainly endeavoured to impress the doctor with a sense of his great danger, and had been laughed at, or cut off with the offer of a pipe, or a plate of fruit. He had been ready to swear a dozen times; only the respect in which he held his cloth had been sufficient to prevent an outbreak. The *doctor* had sworn a dozen times, and more. Yet he had never once lost patience; not even when his guest had pronounced, with tragic vehemence, the "Woe! woe! to them that are at ease in Zion." All he had said in reply was, "*Hell!*" and he had laughed while saying that.

Chapter V

A RED rose bloomed beside the door, and the bees were busy among the honeysuckle trailing the piazza and crowding the windows of the miller's house. Not that the dusty old miller, or his sharp-voiced wife, ever gave a thought to the training of the vines; they were Alicia's; her hand, with the assistance of Al, had put them there, and carefully tended them until they were a bower of bloom, where the bees came summer days, hunting for honey among the pink and pearl white blossoms.

Doctor Boring recognised her spirit everywhere about the picturesque little place the first morning he went to call upon his neighbours. He had felt something like admiration for the miller, as he stood for a moment looking over the gate into the pretty sloping yard with the newly whitewashed cabin in the centre. There was an air of thrift about the place, as if the little mill on the creek had taken its full measure of toll. Even the greens in the garden seemed to have outgrown the vegetables of other gardens. The peas were clambering up their cedar stakes, a riotous jumble of white bloom and delicate tendril. And above the stakes, a glister of gold in the sunlight, he saw Alicia's bright head, beside a slender youth, whom he recognised as "little Al," the delicately disposed brother.

The boy was adjusting some vines that had had a tumble, together with their props. That he found his task an amusing one might be easily inferred from the laughter with which he received Alicia's instructions as to the manner in which the work should be done. More than once she playfully boxed his ears, all unconscious of the visitor regarding them over the palings of the low fence.

The doctor, watching, wondered how many milkmaid castles she had erected upon the proceeds of the truck-patch, when the peas and early potatoes should be ready for the boarding-house at Sewanee.

A smile played about his lips and twinkled for a moment in the eyes that were not always mirrors of mirth, and he playfully shouted:

"Look out for frost!"

Alicia gave a startled little scream, and turned quickly to find the owner of the voice.

Al laughed merrily over her surprise.

"You ware good scared, Lissy, I do believe," said he; "you turned plumb white."

She gave him no reply, if indeed she heard him. She was full of the pleasure of seeing Doctor Boring.

"Come in," she called, "come right in;

the dogs don't bite. I'm awful glad to see you. So'll grandad be, I know. The beans are fullin' right along; you'll get your mess by and by; if, as granny says, 'God spares me.' I certainly think He will, I'm that well and healthy. Though I reckon Brother Barry thinks He ought not to, seein' I'm such a sinner. But sakes! how I do run on, without ever stoppin' to tell you this is my brother, Doctor Borin'. This is Al. I've in and about raised Al; you see he fell to my care when he was just nine years old. Don't you think I've brought him up toler'ble well?"

The laughing face, full a foot above her own, testified to the bringing up, at all events.

"I come mighty nigh outgrowin' my gyardeen," said the boy. "If I keep on I'm mortal certain I'll ketch up with her by and by, doctor."

"But you can't step over that three years' gap between us, son," laughed

Alicia. "No, sir, he ain't anything but a boy dressed up in men's clothes, Doctor Borin'. Don't you mind his grown-up airs; I'm three years older than him, an' I ain't so *mighty* old, as I can make out. He's jist a boy, doctor, that I'm raisin' to take care of me in my old age. Yonder's grandad."

They were walking in single file up the path to the house. An old man, spare, bent, and full of lively interest in the world about him, came out to meet them. Behind him, her sunbonnet about her ears, hobbled granny.

"I'm mighty glad to see you," said grandad. "I've been expectin' of you ever since my granddarter Lissy telled me about yer, an' yer fine fixin's down yander. Lissy she sets store by fine fixin's, *an'* so do I; though you needn't tell the ole woman. Her face air turned heavenward; but me an' Lissy air toler'ble fond o' 'the pomp an' glory,' ain't we, darter? You-uns air valley-born, my granddarter tells me,—come from the town. Well, I'm mount'n, me an' the ole woman. Born, an' lived, an' might 'a' died thar, but for the 'Piscopers. When they took it up we-uns stepped down. But we're mount'n-born. Lissy an' Al air valley; tha'r ma was a valley woman. All well yo' way?"

The doctor laughingly told him that *he* was pretty much all there was "his way," except the servants, the stock, and Zip. "The rest of the family," said he, "enjoy their usual good health."

"Glad to hear it," said the miller. "Glad to hear it. We-uns don't appear ter be as thrivin' as common. Al thar is enjoying mighty poor health lately; he's aguey, threatened o' chills."

"Needs quinine," said the doctor. "Come to see me, Al, and I will give you a tonic that will set you up in a week."

"Hush," whispered the miller; "don't let the ole woman hear you. She don't believe in such; she's goin' ter live an' die by yarbs, an' boneset tea. Thar she air now."

A wrinkled old crone advanced to meet them, peering from under her brown sunbonnet at the visitor. Her eyes were sharp and penetrating; the same might be said of her voice.

"You air the mad doctor, I reckin," she sang out in her cracked treble. "Well, we air all hearty, thank the Lord. Lissy, run an' fetch a cheer for the mad doctor. Maybe he aims to set a spell."

He "set" until near noon, and when he left, it was with a cordial invitation to "come again," and "to be neighbourly."

Lissy walked down to the gate to tell him of another case of fever that had broken out in the village of Pelham. She "wondered if there could be any danger of its making its appearance at S'wanee."

He looked up; the mist-wrapped summits frowned defiance to scourge in any form; the tall tops of the trees swayed lightly in the mountain breeze, itself a tonic to keep at bay the malaria of the lowlands.

"Not up there," said he. "The fever could not live a day up there. That is God's country."

She smiled; a happy, dancing light played among the deeps of her earnest eyes.

"It *air* good," she said, softly, a caress in the slow-spoken words, the dialect of her grandparents, into which she sometimes dropped in her dreamful moods. "It air good an' healthy. I look at it sometimes when the clouds lie low upon it, an' I can only make out the windin's o' the little footpath step by step, an' it seems to me like the hills o' Heavin; an' we can only reach the top of it step by step, ever' day. It certainly *do* seem like the hills of Heavin." She sighed lightly, and rested, her chin upon her hand, her elbow upon the gate, her gaze fixed upon the misty mountain top. "Though," she added, after a moment, "I reckin it'll be a mighty long time befo' I find the hills of Heavin so nigh to hand, — a mighty long time, *if* Brother Barry has the cuttin' of my weddin' garmint. Brother Barry allows I'm give over bodaciously to the *devil*. If, says I, there *be* a devil."

The last sentence was uttered in a whisper, and almost lost in the laugh which accompanied it; a laugh in which the doctor joined as heartily as though the girl had perpetrated some rich joke, rather than scoffed at traditions as old as the hills towering above the cabin in which she was born. Where, he wondered, had the old-fashioned maiden fallen upon the new heresies?

She was a puzzle to him; he studied the puzzle seriously as he tramped home by the brown footpath. She was a careless, happy girl one moment; the next a serious, earnest woman. She could not be more than sixteen years of age, he thought; she was at the turning, the crisis, where girl and woman meet. Careful; careful; oh, how a hand was needed to shape that beautiful young soul! She was full of doubts. Life itself was a wonder, a riddle, to her; it was so beautiful, so fresh, so mysterious. Every fibre of soul and body went to meet it, and trembled and thrilled with the strangeness and the sweetness of it. A word, a hint, would fill her soul with richness; and a word or a hint would crush her peace into ruin for ever. She would make a grand wife; but she was young yet; sixteen.

The doctor opened his door softly, and entered his bedroom. Upon the old-fashioned dresser stood a small square mirror, with his shaving-case lying beside it. He lifted the mirror and carried it to the window; pushed back the white muslin curtain and made a careful study of his face.

"White hair," he said, "may stand for trouble, no less than years. Wrinkles may index sorrow as well as time. And the heart doesn't always keep pace with the body in its race for the grave. Let me see; let me see." He placed the mirror upon the window-sill, and stood looking out, his hands clasped behind his neck, his eyes fixed upon, without seeing, the long reddish lane that led to Pelham. "Forty," he mused, "forty-five and sixteen. Sixteen and ten are twenty-six, and ten are thirty-six, and nine are forty-five. Sixteen from forty-five leaves twenty-nine. It *is* 'a gap,' as she said of the three between her brother and herself. Yet"—

A softness stole into the calm blue eyes; a smile of rare content parted his lips. Had he at last found happiness? That will o' the wisp so many have chased in vain, had it come to him in a cabin under the shadow of the mountains? Truth, freshness, innocence, youth; what else could happiness offer? And to say nothing of the possibilities, the hidden aspirations, and the unsuspected strength that were all to be developed. Life turned its rose again to eyes that had looked upon its sombre side. Hers was a nature easily moved; hers a heart ripe for impressions; her soul one that thirsted for truth, *the* truth. How he would love to have the fashioning of that character, the guiding of the elastic young will. It would be a sweet task,—a very pleasant task indeed. He was half tempted—

He thought of his friends at home; what would they say? Why, that he was mad, stark. But, he reasoned, it was none of their affair. He proposed to live his own life, in his own way, and after his own best interest, as *he* saw it. A strain of an old poem drifted through his thoughts,—a little old song of Browning's. Something had set it jingling in his heart. He repeated it softly, under his breath, the quiet melancholy of his voice lending a charm to the poet's thought:

"The good stars met in your horoscope,
　Made you of spirit, fire, and dew;
　And just because I was thrice as old,
　And our paths in the world diverged so wide,
　Each was naught to each, must I be told?
　We were fellow mortals, naught beside?"

He was fond of Browning, who threw off the conventionalities, broke out of the traces, so to speak, and spoke his thought in his own brave way. The poet reminded him of a fiery horse which, refusing the bit, and spurning alike both chicanery and caress, dies a wild, free thing at last, his great spirit breathed upon and breathing in the untamed children he has sired. Doctor Boring was fond of those untamed children of the poet's brain, and especially fond of Evelyn Hope. And — *was* he fond of Alicia, that he called her "Evelyn" in that low, soft voice of his?

Love is God's great comforter; pain's one consolation; the compensation of all sacrifice; the hope that separates earth from hell; the tie that unites it with heaven. It is the memory of Eden that softens the agony of Gethsemane; it is wiser than Wisdom, richer than Wealth, bolder than Courage, stronger than Death. By a touch it can open the gates of heaven, and with a breath extinguish the fires of torment; it can pave the path to Paradise with rarest gold, — even though that path lie through the sloughs of degradation itself. It speaks to the outcast, and Hope is born; it nestles in the bosom of Despair, and lo! the fires of Faith leap to life again; it grasps the hand of Desolation, and Heaven descends. Only Love is great enough for the great tragedy — Life.

Chapter VI

DOWN the road to Pelham a little cloud of dust arose. It came nearer; the eyes that had been feasting upon visions came back to earth, to see the familiar yellow mule, that had trotted his first patient thither, again stop at the gate. The doctor slipped into his purple gown and went out to meet his visitor, half wondering what manner of prank he would attempt this time. But the man was clothed, even to the afflicted foot, and evidently "in his right mind."

There was something artistic about him; to the very swing of his body swaying gracefully with the movements of the mule. He was clad in his Sunday best, — a coarse, clean shirt and a suit of gray jeans. The inevitable slouch adorned his head; pushed back, it made a kind of setting for the short, clinging curls. Beneath the hat was a face, behind which was hidden a brain that would work out its own problems and stand or fall by its own blunders.

The doctor saw beneath the careless bravado with which his visitor swung himself down from the mule's back and came up the walk to meet him. The large foot touched the ground with positiveness, as if every step took hold upon the solid earth. His eyes were fixed upon the physician; evidently he was not altogether confident as to his reception; but there was that in his manner which said he meant to make the best of things at all events.

"Mornin', doctor," he said in response to the physician's cordial greeting. "I've come over here, Doctor Borin', to pay you a little visit. I'm Joe Bowen, from Pelham Valley down yonder."

The doctor eyed him carefully; it was equally clear to each that the other could scarcely refrain from bursting into laughter.

"Any more erysipelas down your way, Mr. Bowen?" inquired the doctor.

"Oh! say now, Doctor Borin'," said the mountaineer, "you mustn't be holdin' a grudge ag'inst me 'count of that little joke. I'm outright 'shamed of myself about that. Besides, I was only aimin' to plague you a bit — you an' Lissy Reams. Lissy she ware braggin' about you that peart I was afeard, betwixt you, you might git a mortgage on the earth; let alone Georgy. An' Lissy she talked so much that I laid a bet with her as you couldn't tell snake bite from yaller ja'ndice. So when the hornet stung me that mornin', while I was hunt'n' the house over for my boot the coon had carried off, why I —" He broke into laughter in which the doctor was forced to join. "It was *too* comical; it was too damned funny for anything, — ter see you nosin' aroun' an' specticlin' over that toe, an' tappin' of it like it might 'a' been a sp'iled aig, an' allowin' you '*gentlemen* of the medical persuasion' — *ware* it persuasion? or ware it *performance?*— Anyhow, you smart Ikes called it 'erysip'las.'"

The mimicry was so ludicrously perfect the doctor could not speak for laughing. The visitor, too, was enjoying the recital of his smartness, to the utmost; he had enjoyed it before, a score of times and more.

"And blame my hide," he continued, "if that ain't about as nigh the truth as most of yer guesses come. But let that pass. I've come over frien'ly, an' I hope you ain't holdin' no grudge ag'inst me, doctor."

The physician slipped his arm through the arm of his visitor and led him into the house. Grudge? He was at peace with all the world; he had discovered the secret of content; he had awakened to new life, new joy, new hope, "in his old age."

"Grudge!" said he, "grudge, hell! It was a sharp trick you played me, young man. But I shall not refuse to see the fun in it because the joke turned upon me. Come right into my den; there are the pipes on the mantel, and there is a chair for you. The occupant of that old sofa to your left is my chum, Zip. Zip and I are old friends. Fill your pipe; all mountaineers smoke. Most of them drink; if you are ready for a toddy I'll mix one for you."

"I don't drink liquor," said Joe, "but I'll take a turn at the pipe. An' I'm proper proud to make the acquaintance of yer friend here."

He gave the terrier's ear a playful twitch that brought him to his feet and then to the floor, where he stood regarding the visitor in an inquiring way, which sent that worthy off in a peal of laughter.

"Peart pup, to be sure," he said; and, as if the flattery had indeed gone home, the little terrier curled himself at the feet of his new admirer and went to sleep. "No, sir," Joe went back to the previous question, "I don't drink liquor: I can't; it makes a fool of me. A man's an idiot to do that as makes a fool of him, an' beknownst to hisse'f, too. But," he added, with sudden thought, "I ain't got nothin' to say of them that do drink."

"I do not," said the doctor, smiling, while he pressed the brown tobacco into the bowl of his pipe. "I abstain for the same reason that you do; it makes a fool of me; I have no wish to be a greater fool than nature made me."

The mountaineer reached one long calfskin boot to touch the tail of the sleeping terrier:

"Oh, say now! I thought you ware the salt of the earth for smartness. Lissy Reams thinks you air, anyhows."

A smile flitted for a moment about the doctor's lips:

"Does she?" said he, softly. "She is a smart guesser."

"*Does* she? Why, from the way Lissy talks I allowed you an' her would in an' about make a cha'ity hospital of the whole valley bimeby. Why, Lissy says the yarb doctor ain't *nowhar;* that you have got medicine that'll raise the dead out o' their graves — *if* the dead could be induced to swallow it."

The doctor gathered himself to resent the sudden turn the compliment had taken, reconsidered, however, drew in his breath and said, "*The dickens!*"

The mountaineer's eyes twinkled: "But then," he continued, "thar *air* some who say you air nothin' better nor a blamed fool, as never so much as heard of heavin."

He was looking straight into the doctor's eyes; the smoking pipe rested, the bowl in the palm of the broad brown hand. His face was aglow with the amusement felt in reciting the opinions of his neighbours: amusement he saw reflected in the face of his listener, who again took breath and gave expression to a low, half humorous, " Hell ! "

The mountaineer brought his foot down upon the floor with sudden vehemence:

"Say, doctor," he began, "you have heard o' one place, if you haven't heard o' t'other. The valley 'round here, an' the mount'n too, fur that matter, allows that I be the biggest sinner in the State o' Tennessee, or even Georgy hitse'f. But if you ain't toler'ble close behin' me then I ain't no Solerman. Why, they say you never heard o' Christ ! "

The reply was low, earnest, and fraught with meaning:

" Then," said the physician, " they lie."

" Waal, now,"—the mountaineer leaned upon the arm of his chair, his face close to the doctor's. The keen eye of the physician detected a fearless interest, an interest that was not assumed, under the careless, half-merry air with which he demanded, " What do you think of *Him*, anyhow ? "

The doctor removed his pipe from between his lips, tapped the bowl of it gently upon his palm — the tobacco had ceased to smoke in the mountaineer's pipe — and set it upon the hearth, propped against the brass andiron, useless now save for ornament.

"I think," said he, slowly, locking his white fingers loosely upon his knee, and speaking in the quiet tone one unconsciously adopts when talking of the gentle Nazarene, "I think He is my elder brother — and yours."

"Great God!" the boy literally bounded; he gained his feet as if an electric shock had set him upon them. He stood perfectly still one moment, then gave his slouch a shove backward; shook first one leg, then the other, gave the terrier a kick with his calf-clad foot that sent it yelping from the room; then he began pacing up and down, pulling at the fireless pipe in long, deep breaths, never conscious that no wreath of smoke responded to his drawing.

Finally he stopped, looking down at the placid face of the man quietly twirling his thumbs, who had let drop that rank heresy as calmly as though he had expressed himself concerning a rise in Elk River.

"You mean to live *here*," he demanded, "an' preach *that* gospil? Here under the very nose of Brother Barry an' the Episcopers? An' you expect to come out of it whole?—hide, horns, and taller? Great God! You'll find the valley hotter'n hell. You'd as well try to crack Cum'land mount'n wide op'n, as to try to crack the'r skulls wide enough to let in *that* doctrine!"

"I shall not try it," said the doctor. "I came here to get away from creeds and churches, not to build, or to introduce new ones. I shall ask no man to think as I think. I shall neither question nor disturb any man's right to his own belief, and I shall claim the privilege of thinking for myself as well."

His visitor regarded him a moment in a

kind of wonder, not without a touch of admiration. Then he extended his strong, brown hand, palm up. "Put yours thar," he exclaimed. "You have got spunk as well as spare-rib. Blamed if you haven't! Dad burn my hide if I don't jist *admire* the fellow that is too smart for Brother Barry. But, Lord, you don't know *him!*"

"Yes, I do," laughed the doctor. "He called upon me one day last week, and the week before, and the week before that."

"Did he? Come in a mighty big hurry, I reckin; hitched that freckled-faced nag to yo' best apple-tree, *I'll* be bound. Was in a *mighty* hurry an' fluster fixin' of the 'Master's bus'ness;' but made out to let you put up his nag an' *prevail* upon him to stay all night. Oh, I know Brother Barry. He's too durned lazy for man's work, so he tuk to preachin'. An' the way he can preach, while the brethern lay to an' break up his fiel' for him, to keep his family from starvin'! I went over and plowed his gyarden for him las' spring; I done it to pleasure Lissy, more'n anything else. An' when I was in an' about finished, parson he come out an' *threated* me with hell fire if I didn't get religion an' jine his church. You know what I done, Doctor Borin'?"

He stopped, lifted one calfskin and deposited it squarely upon the velvet cushion of the easy chair he had in his excitement vacated, and stood thus, leaning forward, his arm resting upon his knee, his face aglow with enjoyment of the discomfiture of the minister. "I reckin I am an awful sinner," he said; "the worst this side o' torment — thout'n it be you. When Brother Barry thanked me with his slap-jaw talk, I just got aboard o' my yaller mule, an' I says to that holy man, says I: 'Nex' time you wants yo' cussed fiel' broke up do you call on yo' fr'en' the devil to fetch out his spade an' shovel — I have heard he's got one — an ax him to break it up for you. An' if,' says I, 'if you ever come givin' o' me any mo' of yo' jaw I'll break yer darned neck,' says I. I ain't heard from mealy-mouth since then. I ain't lookin' for thanks, Doctor Borin'" (he brought his foot to the floor again), "an' I ain't begrudgin' nobody a little measly day's work at the plow. But I deny a man's right to *drive* a man, even into the kingdom of heaven. I don't believe he'd stay druv after he *ware* druv; sech ain't man natur'— leastwise it ain't my natur'. Nothing won't be druv, if it's half sensed. My grandad druv a drove o' horses through this valley oncet, long ago. An' the last critter of 'em got back again whar they ware druv from. Well, after the cussin' I give him, I reckin he'll let me sa'nter on to ol' Satan at my own gait. I did cuss him; I have that to remember. I may die sometime an' go to the devil, but I have got the satisfaction of knowin' I did perform one good deed in the flesh anyhows."

"What did Lissy say to that?"

"Lissy?" He hesitated, cleared his throat, and blushed to the roots of his yellow hair.

"Yes, Lissy, what did she think of your performance—your one good deed?"

A softness crept into the fearless eyes, lowered now beneath the penetrating gaze of the physician.

"Doctor Borin'," he shifted one great foot nervously, "I tell you, Lissy Reams air a good gal."

"Yes, I know that. That's why I want to know how she received your reckless onslaught upon the church."

There was a moment's embarrassing silence. The clock on the mantel struck the half-past twelve; the keen eyes of the physician were watching every change in the face before him. The mountaineer resumed his seat, awkwardly, and began tugging, with the fingers of his right hand, at the strap of his long boot. The doctor sighed and withdrew his gaze; he was satisfied with that he had discovered.

"Hit's a pity," speech had come at last, since those searching eyes were no longer upon him, " hit's a pity for Lissy to be made a mealy-mouth of. She's a gal o' good sense. She ain't got her own consent to jine the church yit, an' I most hope she won't git it. Lissy is a quare gal, an' if she once takes a stand for the Methodis', thar ain't no tellin' whar it'll end, nor what sort o' fool notions she'll take into her head. She's toler'ble heady for a sensible gal, sometimes. I air goin' to marry Lissy Reams, Doctor Borin'—"

Now it was his turn to look into the doctor's eyes; quick as a flash they fell. If the mountaineer saw anything, if there was anything *to* see, he gave no sign. "I'm goin' to marry Lissy, as soon as little Al's big enough to make a livin' for the ol' folks. I have got a good place t'other side o' Pelham. I can keep Lissy real comf't'ble. Al's fo'teen, goin' on fifteen; Lissy's turned seventeen an' pritty as a pictur'."

Before the doctor could frame a reply old Dilce put her head in to say that dinner was ready — "raidy an' wait'n'."

It was always "ready and waiting" if once old Dilce got it on the table. The two men rose; the doctor laid his hand upon the arm of his guest:

"You are coming out to dinner with me," he said.

But the mountaineer shook his head:

"That's percisely what I ain't," he declared. "I'm not Brother Barry by a long sally. I'm goin' home. An' when you ain't got nothin' better to do, Doctor Borin', you come over to Pelham Valley; you can come the big road or you can keep the path all the way, an' see how a God-forsaken sinner manages to keep his head above water an' starvation. You'll find a pretty lay o' land an' a pleasant pasture, with the creek a-caperin' through it as frisky as it capers for the biggest Methodis' in the State. An' I gits a shower, Doctor Borin', every blessed time my church neighbours gits one. An' if thar's a stint o' sunshine in favour o' they-uns it didn't make itse'f *felt* last July. You come over an' see."

"Will you send me off with dinner on the table?" asked the doctor.

The visitor hesitated, stared, seemed to catch a sudden idea, wheeled about, and, tossing his hat into a corner, said:

"Lead the way. Though God knows I do feel mightily like a Methodis'."

It was sunset when the yellow mule trotted leisurely down the road to Pelham. The physician stood at the gate, watching the big slouch bob up and down with the motion of the animal. When it disappeared in a strip of black gum woods, he placed his hand upon the gate latch, hesitated, dropped it, and turned back slowly to the house.

He had thought of walking down to Lissy's in the dusky twilight. Instead, he went to a little rustic bench under a giant beech, and sat there, lost in thought, until Aunt Dilce called him in to supper. He rose slowly, his hands clasped behind him, and went in.

The lamps had been lighted, and, as he stopped a moment in his sitting-room to make some slight change in his clothing, his eye fell upon the dusty imprint of a gigantic foot upon the velvet cushion of his easy chair.

He smiled and sighed with the same breath. Was he the thoroughly honest fellow he appeared, this young guest of his? It was odd: the visit, the unsought confidence, the breaking of bread in neighbourly way. He had an idea the man had designed to put him on honour not to interfere, so far as Alicia Reams might be concerned, in his love affair.

He sighed again, and passed his hand over his brow as though to remove a veil that had fallen across his vision. His dream had been fast dispelled; life had put on her gloom again. And that when he had but just strangled all doubt, faced and overcome all fear,—just at the moment when he was *about* to be happy. The golden apple had yielded bitter with the very first taste.

Chapter VII

SUMMER drifted dreamily; the valley budded and blossomed, and brought forth its treasures of harvest.

Alicia's peas "fulled" almost to bursting in their pale pods, and the shrivelled vines were torn away to make room for a turnip patch, in order that "spring greens" might not be lacking when the season for them should come again. Still the physician tarried. Autumn, with its variant winds and restful skies, breathed upon field and flood; the water sank low in the Elk's bed, and the rebellious creek crooned the old, old slumber song of October; the wild grape hung in dusky bunches from the vine-crowned trees; the stealthy fox prowled along the river bluffs that were rich with the odour of the ripening muscadine; the mountaineer fed upon the opossum that had fattened upon the new persimmons. And still the doctor let fall no hint of returning to the city.

Autumn gave place to winter; the water rose in the river channel, and the foot log went scurrying off with the swollen waters of Pelham Creek. The birds gathered in little frightened groups, made out a hasty route, and went south on very short notice. Only a dilapidated crow might be heard now and then, monotonously cawing from the tops of a denuded sycamore-tree. There was an occasional dropping of dry nuts from the limbs where they had clung all summer, seeking the moist brown earth to wait until — Ah! who knows when, how, what shall rise again?

At last the snow came; little drowsy dribbles that frosted the hills and put a crisp in the air. And still the good man lingered.

"Why should I go?" he asked himself. "I am contented here; am doing a little good, maybe, among the people here."

He scarcely knew himself that Alicia had anything to do with his staying; he scarcely understood just how he felt towards her.

He saw her almost every day; if she failed to call, he hailed her when she passed, taking the nearer cut, the footpath way to Sewanee. For in winter, also, Alicia found something with which to tempt the appetites of the "Episcopers."

As for the doctor, his cheery call at the miller's gate had become as familiar as the click-clack of the mill itself. And so frequent were his demands for "more eggs" that granny fell to wondering "if the mad doctor ware a-feedin' of his cows an' horses on Lissy's hens' aigs."

It was one afternoon in November that he returned from a visit to a sick man down the valley. He was tired; his very eyes ached with wind that had cut him unmercifully as he rode home in the teeth of it. He drew off his boots, stretched his chilled feet a moment before the fire, and thrust them into a pair of felt slippers with a sense of quiet rejoicing that he was home ahead of the snow cloud gathering over the mountain. The fire had never felt so good. Even Zip, as he curled up at his feet, his small head cuddled against the brown felt shoe, assumed vaguely the semblance of a friend.

He had scarcely had his first yawn when Dilce put her head in to say:

"Marster, dey's a 'oman sick up dar on de mount'n road a piece: mighty sick; en ole Mis' Reamses granddaughter wuz down here after you whilst you wuz gone. En she say she ud tek it mighty kin' ef 't you'ud step up dar en see de 'oman what's sick. She say ef't you could come dis ebenin' she ud be mighty obleeged ter yer. But I tol' her you wan' gwine do no sich thing, not in dis col' en win'."

He tossed off his slippers but a moment before put on, and, pointing to his boots still lying where he had but just left them, said:

"Who is the sick woman? Did Lissy leave no name?"

"Naw, sir. I axed fur the entitlements, but she didn't look lack she cud make out what dey wuz."

"No," said the doctor, "I suppose not; hand me my shoes, you villainous murderer of the king's English. Now tell me what the girl *did* say. You don't expect me to go tramping up the mountain into the clouds, with nothing nearer than the stars for a sign-post, do you?"

"She say hit's de fus' house on de road, after you tu'n de road by de big rock what hangs over hit, whar de S'wany boys hab painted de sun risin'. Mus'n' I git yo' supper fus' fo' you goes out again in de col'?" she asked, seeing him look about for his greatcoat. "I kin hab it on de table in a minute."

"No," he said, wearily, "wait until I get back, or get your own, and keep mine back in the stove. I am going up by way of the foot-path, but you may give Ephraim his supper and then send him with my horse around by the road."

"Marster?"

"Well?"

"Hadn' I better fix up a bite fur yer ter carry up dar? Mis' Reamses daughter say dat de sick 'oman's folks is all gone 'way, an' she wuz 'bliged ter g'long back up dar ter knock her up somef'n ter eat. She say she got de mis'ry in de side, mighty bad."

"You may get me a box of mustard, and when Ephraim comes send a basket of provisions up. You had better put a bottle of blackberry wine in the basket, also. And tell Ephraim to get in plenty of wood; there is going to be a snow-storm."

The atmosphere cleared, however; the snow ceased to fall; and, although it was nearing the hour of sunset when he reached the cabin on the mountain's side, there was a deep, half-sullen glow in the west which brought out all the more forcefully the otherwise cold gray of the heavens.

He found the sick woman to be old Mrs. Tucker, whom he had met at the cabin where he first met Alicia; he had bought chickens of her more than once since then; and her son, a listless, idle fellow with a young wife and a baby, had hauled wood for the physician from the forests upon the mountain. He had no idea that he would ever be paid for his services, if that payment depended upon the son. There was, however, something about the old woman herself, hints of those peculiarly strong and admirable characteristics which flash upon the comprehension with startling emphasis at times, that had inspired him with faith as well as respect.

The tumble-down gate swung slightly ajar upon a broken hinge; a tiny line of blue smoke was ascending from the low stack chimney, and in the woods, across the road, a young girl was gathering brush.

He did not recognise her at first in the half light, but when she pushed back the shawl pinned about her head and came to meet him, he saw that it was Alicia.

"I'm mighty glad you're come, Doctor Borin'," she said, in her slow, sweet drawl. "I was most afraid you wouldn't, because Aunt Dilce said you were off to see some one already. Come right on in; it's old Mis' Tucker that's sick, and her folks air all off visitin' down to Pelham."

She was trying to open the hanging gate by pushing against it with her already burdened arms. The doctor put her lightly aside.

"Wait, wait, young woman," said he. "Don't monopolise the work, I beg. Let me open the gate, or else carry the brush."

It scraped along the frozen ground like a thing in pain, digging a long furrow in the light snow-crust as it went.

"Her folks air all gone off," Lissy was

telling him as they walked towards the cabin, "else I reckin they wouldn't 'a' let me send for you. Jim he's mighty strong for the herb doctor, an' so is Lucy Ann; but I have heard Mis' Tucker passin' compliments over you so many times that I up and went after you this evenin' without askin' leave of nobody, just on the strength of them compliments."

"Much obliged, I'm sure," said the doctor, "much obliged to both of you."

She did not detect the jest in his words, and her simple "You are welcome," as she led the way into the cabin, was as genuinely sincere as it was quaintly simple.

She deposited her kindlings in the shed-room, and returned to take her place with him at the bedside of old Mrs. Tucker.

To him there was no longer anything odd or incongruous in her being there. He had found her so often among the very poor and the suffering, so many times had they been thus associated together, that it seemed as much her proper place as it was his. She was as truly a physician to them as he.

"Had she been a poor girl, in a city, she would have been a trained nurse," was his thought; "had she been a rich woman, in the city, she would have been a patron of hospitals, with the afflicted indigent for a hobby. As it is, she ought to be a doctor's wife," and, so saying, blushed to the roots of his gray hair.

Old Mrs. Tucker, however, received more of Alicia's attention than the general sick. The two had been real friends since Alicia, a little girl in short skirts, had made her first trip to Sewanee behind Mrs. Tucker on her gray mare. She had sold a mess of early beans that day, and with Mrs. Tucker's help had purchased a straw hat with the money. It was the very first hat she had ever owned; but since then so much from spring and fall vegetables was invested in a hat. The last winter's was a bright red felt, which the old grandmother declared made her look for all the world like an overgrown woodpecker. Mrs. Tucker liked it, however, and the face that peeped at Lissy from the little mirror over the bureau that had been her mother's was such a piquant, pretty face, under the red felt's brim, that she had worn it, in defiance of the woodpecker insinuation. The hat was in the second season now, but still retained its bright red colour; so that when Lissy crammed it down upon her head and started up the mountain on a clear day in winter, it showed like a scarlet flag "plumb to the top of the mount'n," Mrs. Tucker was wont to declare.

Alicia seldom passed the cabin without stopping to ask after the health of the family. Thus it was that she found the old woman ill, with a chill upon her, and alone.

"She was right glad to see me," she

told the doctor, while she stroked the thin black hair from the yellow forehead. "But I didn't ask her if I might send for you, Doctor Borin'. And if any harm comes of it the fault's all mine—if any harm comes to Mis' Tucker."

The doctor caught his breath, looking up quickly to discover, if might be the insult was of accident or intent.

But the quiet face told nothing; Alicia went on stroking the yellow temples as calmly as though she had not just put the physician on his honour to play no "infedel tricks," as her grandmother was wont to call his practice, upon the patient committed to his care.

Without replying, he proceeded to examine the sufferer, who waked and recognised him, telling him that she was "much obleeged to him for trompin' up the mount'n ter see a ole woman die."

"Nonsense," said he. "You will bring me my Christmas turkey ten years from now, if Lissy will swing her kettle over the fire, and get some hot water to put your feet in. Then she must hunt up a saucer in which to mix a little mustard, and get for me a bit of soft *cotton* cloth. I am going to put a plaster on your side, and another on your chest. And I am going to give you a little powder out of this case,— it is called *quinine*. Lissy?"

She turned to him from the fire where she had been swinging the kettle upon an iron hook that was there for the purpose.

"Will you be here all night?"

"I reckin I'll have to be," she replied. "Though some one ought to go down to Pelham and let Lucy Ann and Jim know their ma is sick. I'll be obliged to run down the mount'n and feed my chickens first, because Al *won't* give 'em enough, and granny plumb forgets all about 'em. Then I can come back."

She sighed, standing with her hands

folded, her profile against the blaze, her fine, clear-cut face and figure silhouetted against the firelight.

"It's mighty worrisome to know somethin' is left to your care; something that can feel, and suffer, and die; though," she added, with a smile, "it be only a brood of chickens."

He went over and stood by her side, looking down into the earnest young face lifted to his.

"What if the 'something' be human life?" he said, softly; "what if it rested in your hand every day, almost every hour? What would you think of such a charge as that?"

Her lids dropped for a moment; she hesitated, then, looking at him with strangely glowing eyes, said:

"Oh, it must be *grand, grand,* to help people to live, — to know how to give 'em back their life. It *is* grand. It is like God, to be able to do that. To give back life, and to help people to live their life after they get it; I'd like mightily to be able to do that."

Her face was aglow with enthusiasm; the fine lights sparkled in her eyes like crystalline fires.

She was very near him, her hand resting upon the back of a splint-bottomed chair which stood between them. She leaned forward, resting her elbows upon the chair, waiting for him to speak. He could feel her soft breath upon his hand; see the throbbing of her white throat; and the pretty bird-like neck, where the waist of her dark dress had been cut back to make room for a tiny ruffle of white muslin. He saw the rise and fall of her bosom; her gold-red hair brushed his sleeve. The firelight transfigured her; the dress of dark stuff, in the ruddy, uncertain light, became softest velvet; the brooch of cheap glass, at her throat, became a glistening gem of rarest worth. The fluffy bright waves of hair that crowned the well-shaped head were not for the rude caresses of the mountain stripling, Joe Bowen; they were his, the treasured tresses of his love, Alicia; his wife that might be.

His wife that might be for the asking. He knew her heart had not wakened; all the sweet beauty of life's richness was still there. It would never be called into being by Joe Bowen. The girl had a soul; Bowen's was not the voice that would sound its quickening. Yet unless he spoke she would marry him, and the great richness, the wonderful possibilities, would be lost, all lost.

He leaned slightly towards her, his hand rested upon hers; he felt the slender, flexible fingers close about his own.

"Alicia?" he said, softly.

She started, and withdrew her hand. He knew then that her thoughts had been far away.

"Alicia, how would you like to help the world? in what manner, I mean?

And where did you get your idea of being of service to your fellows?"

"At S'wany," she replied. "I was up there once of a Sunday. I didn't care much for the robe and fixin's of the preacher — seemed like they was no use. But I remembered what he said. He said we couldn't all be rich and smart; no more could we all see our way clear; but we all could help somebody to live their life, somebody not so well off as we air. He said we could all do somethin', even if we couldn't understand God; and He would count the good up to our credit. He said we could make our fellow men our religion, and helpin' of them our creed. I got that much from the Episcopers, and I'm tryin' to live up to it. Doctor Borin', I *have* thought that was true religion."

"It will do to steer by, I suspect," he replied. "But some day I want to come over to your house and plan out a future for you, more congenial than this life you have laid out for yourself."

She laughed and lifted the steaming kettle from the hook to the hearth. Her next words were foreign to his suggestion.

"Doctor Borin,' if you could stay here a bit I could run down and feed my chickens, and get back in no time."

Already her hand was extended for her shawl hanging upon a wooden peg just within the cabin door.

"Child," said the doctor, "what are you made of? Rubber or whitleather? Talking of slipping down the mountain as though you were a couple of cast-iron springs, and had only to snap yourself in place. You have been down the mountain once to-day."

She laughed, and tossed a handful of chips in the fire, from the basket she had filled for the morning's kindling.

"I have been down the mountain *twicet* to-day," she said, "but I can go again, I reckon. And I don't know but I *ought* to go down to Pelham and tell Lucy Ann."

"Well, you'll not go to Pelham this night," said the doctor. "My horse and boy will be around in half an hour, and, if you will direct him to the house where Lucy Ann is stopping, he can go down there and tell her that she is needed here. You may go and feed your chickens, if you are so sure nobody can perform the service to your satisfaction. Has Lucy Ann any way of getting home to-night?"

"They went down in the wagon," she replied. "Jim he had a load of straw to fetch up, for bed-makin' and hen nests; and he allowed Lucy Ann and the baby could ride on the load well as not."

Half an hour later Ephraim had been sent upon his mission, and Doctor Boring saw Alicia cram her old red felt down upon her head, pin her shawl securely about her shoulders, and run down the little footpath that wound past his own dwelling to hers, at the foot of the mountain.

It was scarcely ten minutes until he

heard her voice at the gate again, and through the curtainless window he could distinguish in the fading light the slight, girlish figure leaning upon the low palings, on the other side of which stood a tall, slender youth, whose erect carriage, and shock of yellow hair falling picturesquely about his shoulders, and surmounted by the inevitable slouch, proclaimed him no other than Joe Bowen. His head drooped, ever so slightly, to meet the pretty face lifted to his. She was laying down instructions of some kind, for the giant nodded now and then, and her pretty, gurgling laugh, half suppressed, in consideration of the sick woman, came to the ears of the physician, watching and listening, with a feeling half anger, half annoyance, in his heart, until the conference was ended and Lissy returned to her charge.

"Is she asleep?" she asked, softly, while she laid aside her things. "I met Joe Bowen yonder where the path forks, and he said he'd go down and feed the chickens for me. Joe's a master hand at chickens, though he *is* a sinner."

She laughed, tucking the covers more securely about the feet of her patient. Evidently Joe's sins were not altogether unpardonable to her partial sense.

"But," she added, naïvely, "I ain't so mighty good myse'f as I can be settin' myse'f in judgment on Joe. I ain't a perfessor; I ain't even clear in my mind that I believe all the Methodists say; nor the Episcopers either, for that matter. I know there ain't any sense in all that talkin' back at the parson like the Episcopers talk, same as if he didn't know what he was sayin'; an' there ain't any call for him to put on them robe fixin's as I can see. And all of that about the dead risin' I know ain't so. For Joe opened an Indian grave last summer—there's a whole graveyard of 'em over yonder on Duck River—and there was the Indian dead and buried same as ever.

And he must 'a' been buried a hundred years I know. Oh,"— she paused; a new idea had come to her,—"mebby the Indians don't count. The Book don't say anything about Indians, and neither does Brother Barry. Air you goin'?"

"Yes, I must get down the mountain while I can see the path. I am not as young as I used to be."

She laughed again, and toyed with the pewter spoon and coarse saucer with which he had prepared the mustard.

"You don't appear to be so mighty old, as I can make out," she said.

The words pleased him. Age had never been unwelcome to him; in fact, he had scarcely felt that it had really come to him, until he crossed paths with this pure young life. Her very next words, however, served to dash the little sweet with bitter.

"Are you afraid to remain here alone?" he asked. "If you are, I will send Aunt

Dilce up to stay with you. Mrs. Tucker will not waken before midnight possibly; I have given her a sleeping potion."

There was the faintest hint of embarrassment in her manner as she replied:

"Joe said he'd come up and sit with me till Lucy Ann got here, and then he said he'd fetch me home again."

"Oh! he did!"

There was a slight impatience in the words, but she did not recognise it. She was innocent of intent to wound; too unconscious of offence, too entirely unused to the world and its ways, to understand that she could be in any sense a cause, however innocent, of contention,—a thorn in the bosom of a man's content.

She gave him her earnest and entire attention while he explained the different medicines and gave directions concerning them, interrupting him now and then, if it might be called an interruption, with her simple "Yes, sir," "No, sir," "All right, Doctor Borin'." She even walked to the gate with him, and put the rusted chain over the post that held the broken fastenings; and called to him as he went off down the snow-dusted path:

"I'll fetch you a basket of fresh eggs to-morrow, sure and certain."

And he had called back to her, "So do; so do," quite cheerily.

Yet there was an ache in his heart; the thorn had pierced home.

Chapter VIII

THE patient was asleep and Alicia busy putting things to rights in the shed-room, when Joe tapped upon the window. Carefully she opened the door to admit him, and drew back, laughing noiselessly at the figure he presented. His arms were filled with the hickory sticks that he had cut in the forest; his very chin was invisible; only a mass of tawny hair, a slouch, and a pair of restless blue eyes appeared above the "lumber pile."

"I fetched you up an armful of wood," said he. "I'll pile it back here by the fireplace handy for you. I reckin it won't come amiss in the mornin', nohow."

"Set it down careful, Joe," said Lissy, "so's not to disturb Mis' Tucker. It was certainly thoughtful of you to fetch it up for — Lucy Ann."

"Lucy Ann be —"

"Heish," laughed Lissy, nodding towards the sick-room.

"Waal," said Joe, "I didn't fetch it for *her*, though I knew in reason she'd use it. I reckin I'd better take the pail and run down to the spring for some water. It's goin' to be mighty dark outside, an' toler'ble cold. Yes, I lay I'll fetch a pail o' water — for Lucy Ann."

Alicia left the dishes she was arranging on their shelves, and came and stood by him, resting her hand lightly upon his sleeve.

"You're mighty good, Joe," she said, "an' mighty thoughtful o' others."

He looked down into the pretty, uplifted face so near his shoulder. It was very pleasant to have the face there — very pleasant.

"I'm afeard it's only you I'm thinkin' of, Lissy," he admitted. "A feller don't deserve much praise for tryin' to pleasure the girl he loves, I reckin. But —" he hesitated; it was pleasant to hear from Alicia's pretty mouth that he was "good;" he would like her to say it again, to have her think it always; but his natural honesty spurned the deceit. "Shucks!" he said, "I ain't 'good.' You know I'm the biggest sinner on this earth, maybe in Georgy, too. Ask old mealy-mouth, if you misdoubt it, — he'll tell you, Brother Barry will. Shucks! I say I'd ruther be a sinner o' the deepest dye 'an ter be like him; he's the darndest —"

She laid her hand lightly upon his lips:

"Heish!" The laughter in her eyes belied the sternness in her voice. "You're mighty wicked, that's certain; and I ain't any better. I reckin we're about give over to Satan alike, — me and you, and Doctor Borin', too."

There was a momentary flash in the eyes fixed upon her. If she saw it, it was gone so quickly she doubted it had been there; his voice was friendly enough when he asked, quietly:

"Has he been here, the mad doctor?"

"Why, I went after him," she replied, "and he wasn't there, but he come up and fixed a plaster out o' mustard, and mixed somethin' in a teacup, for Mis' Tucker to swallow; and then he went home again. O Joe, I just wish you could hear him say—" she glanced over her shoulder, drew closer to his side, and put her lips to his ear—"'Hell!' when things don't go to pleasure him."

"I heard him say a hornet sting ware erysip'las," said Joe, mollified by the nearness of her face, "an' if I rickerlict right hit ware me as said 'Hell' that time."

"I'll be boun' it was," said Alicia. "When compliments o' that kind air passin' I'll be boun' you'll get in a say. What's become o' the pail o' water, Joe? I reckin I'll need it about knockin' up somethin' for Lucy Ann and Jim to eat, 'gainst they get here."

"Plumb forgot it," said Joe. "But I'll go now, if I can get my own consent ter tear myse'f away ter the spring an' leave you a-standin' here by yourse'f when I might be a-standin' with you."

She glanced up with sudden inspiration.

"Why, Joe," she said, "I'll go with you. Wait till I peep at Mis' Tucker."

She drew the covers gently about the sleeper, noiselessly laid a stick of wood on the fire, and as noiselessly slipped back to Joe, the cedar water-bucket in one hand, her old shawl in the other.

"I'll have to hurry back and get you a mouthful to eat," she said, as they started briskly off together.

"Don't you be worryin' about me," said Joe. "I come over here ter he'p you, not to be makin' of more work for you-uns; I can just as well wait till the rest have their supper as not, and waitin' will make less work for you, Lissy. My! this gate *is* a bother; I'll come over ter-morrer an' mend it, if the Lord spares me, seein' as that lazy Jim won't. Now then! see who'll get ter the spring first."

They swung the bucket between them, and started off, like two children, in the crisp, cold air, down the road to the spring under the bluff's side. It was a short run, for there was no moon, and the stars were straggling in the west, clouds were gathering, and when they turned off the road into the foot-path, the way was too narrow, and the rattling dead undergrowth too close and thick, for further racing. They tarried but a moment, for the night was cold; yet they returned slowly, and their talk was serious, their voices low, as if that had been said at the spring under the bluff which had touched the stronger chords and awakened the deeper feelings of the heart. In his right hand Joe carried the bucket; his left lay upon his heart, and Lissy's right slipped through his arm was snugly folded within it.

"I'm a-comin' sometime, *sometime*," she was saying; "just as soon as they can spare me. When you talk about the little chickens and the lambs, and the cows waitin' to be milked, I want to go real bad, and he'p you with 'em, Joe. I like little chickens; and I never hear a lamb bleat but I want to pick it up in my arms and rock it to sleep. But—"

She hesitated, and, resting her head against his arm, sighed.

"Do as you see best, Lissy," said Joe. "I'm a-tryin' not ter worry you. But it do seem to me as you air mighty give ter puttin' off."

"I know it," she admitted. "I know it, Joe. Granny's tellin' me about that constant; and Brother Barry."

"Oh, damn Brother Barry! What's old mealy-mouth got ter do with you-uns? I know I do despise the groun' he tromps on. An' I tell you now, Lissy, I ruther hear that ole sinner down yander, the mad doctor, as don't know heaven from hornet—I'd ruther hear him draw his breath in an' shet his teeth, an' say one good honest 'Hell!' like he says it, as to hear Brother Barry hallelu-yahin' for a month. Thar's more religion in it, ter *my* notion. An' thar' ain't no sneak about him, nuther. He's ready ter own up, fair and square, if a feller gits the best of him. Why, he told it all over the mount'n about that hornet-sting joke, — told it up ter S'wanee even; let on he ware plumb sold. It was only a little runt of a joke anyhow; but blamed if he didn't stan' up ter it like a man."

"I reckin we're all mighty wicked," said Lissy, ignoring the bringing of the doctor into the conversation; "but somehow I can't bring myse'f to think like Brother Barry. I can't make God out to be as Brother Barry makes Him. He preached to the people over at Goshen last fall that God killed Ike Jordan last September, because Ike drove his sheep up the mountain on Sunday. Everybody knew the lightnin' struck him when he was bringin' Mis' Tucker's warpin' bars home for her, because she wasn't able to git a wagon and go down to Pelham to get 'em, and there was nobody else at home to go, unless it was Lucy Ann's baby, that hadn't learned to walk yet. And he told at Jim Tyler's funeral last spring that the Lord had need of Jim and took him home. I'm a-thinkin' as they must be a mighty sca'ce of hands in heaven if such a no-'count as Jim Tyler was needed to fill out. Truth is, Jim fell off the bluff when he was drunk and broke his own neck, after gettin' lost goin' home from Tracy. He was a professin' member, however, and so maybe his sprees ware overlooked, and he really had a call to come up higher.

"I'm a sinner, — I can't set myse'f up in judgment. Though it always seemed to me as there ought to be, as there *must* be, some better way o' savin' folks than by threat'nin' of 'em, an' killin' 'em off with lightnin' and such. Seems like it ain't right; it makes God most like a —

wild beast. I reckin that's why I can't love Him; I'm 'fraid of Him. An' I won't be druv — I can't. But I would truly like to know, for certain; I'd like to know what *be* the truth. Sometimes I almost get my own consent to ask Doctor Borin' to tell me."

The arm upon which her hand rested gave a sudden jerk; the owner of it stood free of her, and, although it was too dark for her to see his face, she understood that Joe was angry; the jealousy that had been brooding in his heart suddenly burst forth.

"Do!" he exclaimed, "do ask him; he knows; he knows ever'thing. He's smart — he's smart as God, I reckin; since he knows the plan o' salvation so peart. Keeps it corked up like he does his doctor stuff, in a bottle, I reckin. Oh, yes! go ask the mad doctor to save yo' soul; he can do it. He'd like mighty well to have you saaft-so'derin' him like the *sisters* saaft-so'der Brother Barry.

An' it ain't so clear ter my mind but you'd enjoy it 'bout as much as old erysip'las would."

"Joe Bowen!"

Her voice was full of surprised indignation; had he been calmer, more himself, he would have known that he alone had suggested Doctor Boring, as something more than the truly benevolent friend, the lonely old man, the thoroughly good physician. He would have detected in her simple, startled exclamation, her inability to find words with which to deny his unseemly charge, the very first intimation of the doctor's regard for her that had ever so much as hinted itself to her unsuspecting heart. But he was too angry to see anything, or to heed what he did or said.

"Oh, I know you, Lissy," he broke out, fiercely. "You're mighty *keerful* not ter set a day for marryin' me; I'll lay you wouldn't find it so hard ter fix a time for marryin' him, if he asks you. I know you. It's all mighty well ter be runnin' over the mount'n nussin' of the sick, as ain't no manner o' kin ter you, an' got no manner o' claim, when you know *he'll* be thar, ter pass compliments over you, an' send you off ter breakfast at *his* house, ridin' *his* horse. An' happen he ain't thar you must up an' *sen'* for him ter *mix mustard*, an' dose out *qui-nine;* an' do a lot o' rubbish that ain't got neither sense nor savin' in it. Darn his hide! if he don't leave this valley I'll shoot him. An' you may tell him so with my compliments. Shucks! it's easy as eatin' ter see he's in love with you."

They had reached the door of the shed-room; Lissy stood with her hand upon the latch-string, afraid to draw it, lest the loud, angry voice disturb the sick woman in the next room. Yet she was terribly angry; angry enough to go in at that door and leave him there on the outside, and on the outside of her life, for ever. She had made no reply to his outbreak other than the simple exclamation of surprise. While she stood there, waiting until he should finish his tirade, she heard Mrs. Tucker calling to her to come in: "she wanted her special."

"Mis' Tucker's 'wake and wantin' me," she said, quietly. "Good-night, Joe. You can leave the pail outside, I sha'n't need it." And giving the latch-string a pull, she went in, and left him there in the darkness, with the door shut fast between them.

He had planted a thought in her heart that might never be cast out; had accomplished that which, of all things, he would not have done. He had awakened her wonder, drawn for her a comparison between himself and the man sleeping at that moment the sleep of one who feels that he has met a burden and lifted it; — he had lifted many burdens for the poor; the last for the old woman to whose need he had responded at the sacrifice of his own comfort and inclination. Joe, too, had offered his shoulder to the burden; but, ah, the difference of motives. He admitted that difference to his own heart as he rode through the valley towards his home. But he was ungenerous enough to hope that Alicia would not see it in the same light.

But Alicia scarcely thought of him. At another time, girl-like, she would have sat down and cried over the ruin of her pretty dream; but now, having explained to Mrs. Tucker that Joe had "got mad and gone home," and having given her the medicine as she had been instructed to give it, and having seen her patient drop into a gentle slumber, Alicia went back to the shed-room, made a pot of coffee for Lucy Ann and Jim, and otherwise proceeded to "have things ready 'gainst their comin'."

But that night, when her work was done, and the pretty head lay upon its pillow in Mrs. Tucker's close little rafter room, sleep, heretofore so easily wooed, refused to come. Still, her thoughts were not of Joe, so much as of Joe's words. *Did* the doctor care for her? She felt the red creep to her temples. She had never thought of such a thing; but now — since Joe had thought for her — his touch had been always gentle, his voice *ever* kind; he had always a smile for her. "And he was so good; he never went off at a tangent and railed out upon folks. If he loved a woman, and knew some one else loved her better, he would close his lips for all words but the very kindest. He would never fault a girl because some one else found her good and pretty."

And although no word was spoken, Joe lost by comparison.

"It did look bad, perhaps, her always meeting him when there was sickness;" so ran her thought; "but she had always helped this way. Most of the neighbours did, who had nothing to prevent. Still, it did look bad; she had never thought of it before, but now that she did think, it looked decidedly queer. She would not do it again. Doctor Boring might think bad of it his own self—might think she was trying to meet him. And she wouldn't go over there as free as she had been going; he might think bad of that. But, no; he was good; had sense; he was too good to think bad of anybody. And he liked her to come, ordered eggs just to make her come — perhaps." And with a smile upon her lips, as if the thought might be not altogether unpleasant, Alicia fell asleep.

Chapter IX

THERE was trouble in the wind. The old trust, the quiet sense of oneness that had existed between Joe and Lissy, had received a shock. As the weeks went by and the quarrel was not made up, Joe began to grow sullen and morose. He had never known Lissy as she appeared to him during those weeks. Light, gay, careless, she seemed to care no more for his anger than she cared for his suffering. He had expected to teach her a lesson, to force her to sue for forgiveness; failing in that, he sought to play upon her tenderness, to reach her by his own sadness and regret.

His first call after the rupture was ostensibly upon the old people. He brought a turn of corn to the mill, and while waiting "allowed he'd step up ter the house an' see how granny was comin' on."

Lissy saw him coming up the mill path, and, blushing, rose to receive him. After all, she liked Joe, and regretted the quarrel! had he asked her to do so, at that moment of surprise and pleasure, she might have received him again into her trust and affection.

But he merely gave her a careless "Howdy, Lissy," and asked to see her grandmother.

The next time he called she was careful to meet him at the door, and, calling to her grandmother that he was there, went quietly on making her preparations for carrying some fresh butter to the boarding-house on the mountain. He had the chagrin of seeing her adjust the red felt upon her head with more than her usual care; she even tied a bit of bright ribbon into her hair; he noticed how perfectly the red adornment blended with the color in her cheek; and he noticed, in the same mirror that had reflected the laughing, girlish face, his own hollow eyes, telling the story of sleepless nights and weary vigils. She made no apology for leaving; on the contrary, she tossed him an offhand defiance by calling to Al to bring her the basket of eggs for Doctor Boring.

"I'll stop as I go by, and see if anybody's sick and needin' me," she said. "I'm gettin' my hand out since Mis' Tucker got up and about. Though I'm glad she's well, goodness knows. Well, an' singin' the praises of the mad doctor like the woods afire."

Granny unconsciously added fuel to the flame jealousy had kindled:

"Though she's a-wonderin' some whar the pay air ter come from, for the powders an' stuff he give her. It do beat my time, the hold the infidel air gittin' on the valley. He even tol' Lissy thar as he'd make his nigger plow her gyarden, an' plant it, in the spring. Sowin' ter destruction, I tell Lissy, but seems like her an' her grandad can't see it so."

Joe could do nothing but see her go off with that contented look upon her face, and a basket on either arm.

But his visit lost its flavour when she was gone; he had exhausted himself upon the new colt he had bought and meant to "break ter a side-saddle," before Alicia left; the horse was mean and valueless enough when it dawned upon him that the rider he had intended should occupy that same side-saddle might never mount it, after all,— might marry the mad doctor, just to spite *him;* for it never occurred to him that she could really love the man old enough to be her father. Still she might marry him; women were guilty of very foolish acts sometimes, and Lissy was a woman. So he reasoned, and the more he reasoned the more angry he became; until, unable to sit tamely there with the knowledge that she was at that moment at his rival's house, sitting opposite him at the fire perhaps, with that same motherly sweetness in her face that had been there when she spoke of rocking the little lambs to sleep in her arms, he got up, said good-by, and struck out across the mountain. He meant to meet her somewhere upon the way, or to wait for her if she tarried, and to have it out with her. They must either "make it up" or "fight it out," he declared; meaning that she was to understand that she couldn't play fast and loose with him.

By the time he reached Mrs. Tucker's cabin his anger had cooled somewhat; he was quite willing to make up. *If* Alicia would agree to marry him without further "foolishness," or would even "fix a day," however distant, he would let "bygones be bygones and say no more about it." So he hung about, talking to old Mrs. Tucker, and inwardly fretting because Alicia tarried at the doctor's.

When at last she did come she would have passed him without a word, without so much as a nod of recognition, but that he went down the road a little distance to meet her. Then when her eyes were lifted to his he saw that she had been weeping; the lids were instantly drooped, refusing to meet his.

Old Mrs. Tucker from her window could see, without hearing what was said, that Joe was angry. She saw, too, that which Joe failed to see, — that Alicia was not feigning indifference.

As they drew nearer, her sharp old ears caught a threat the jealous young lover let fall; not the whole of it, but enough to convince her that the doctor was in danger of his life.

"Land o' mercy!" she exclaimed. "Air Joe Bowen drunk? Or air he out of his head? *Or* air he just a nat'ral fool? Jealous of the mad doctor! Well, I'll be beat! What air we-all a-comin' ter, I wonder. Thar! if Lissy ain't comin' in, an' just leavin' him ter preach ter the gate-post an' the horse-block. I don't wonder. I ain't forgot how he talked that night I ware so sick, an' I called the child in so's he couldn't jaw the life out of her, — though he didn't know I heard his threatn'n', an' no more did Lissy."

How easy it would have been to set him right; yet Alicia refused to speak the consent he asked, or to explain her tears and agitation. She had meant to tell him, to be kind to him; but he had given her no opportunity; now she said "he might go."

She gave Mrs. Tucker a quiet "Good-mornin'," and as that woman wisely refrained from speaking of the quarrel, it was not mentioned.

After awhile she said "Good-mornin'" again, and went back down the mountain, home, and sent Al to carry the butter to Sewanee. Once alone in her own little room with its white naked walls and muslin curtains, Alicia buried her face in the pillows of her bed and burst into tears. For the moment, Joe became dear; the sense of loss made him so. But the next day she went about her duties as usual; the storm had passed. Of his threats she had little fear. She had known him a long time, almost all her life, and she had never known him do a cowardly or an unprincipled thing. She could say that much for him, at all events.

Mrs. Tucker, however, was not so sure of him. No sooner had Alicia gone home than the old woman tied the strings of her black sunbonnet under her chin and went down the mountain. She did not follow the footpath leading to the physician's house from the rear, but took the little trail to the right which would cross the "big road" at a point where she knew he often walked mornings, going as far, sometimes, as Pelham Creek.

When she reached the top of a little bluff where there was a clearing, she saw him coming down the road, flecking with his cane at the long dry grasses either side. His head was dropped forward in the attitude of one lost in thought. And indeed, he had abundant cause for meditation; he was half tempted to close his house and go back to the city, as his first plan had been, and remain there until summer. Joe Bowen was beginning to annoy him considerably. He had been disappointed in Bowen; he had not been the friend a first acquaintance with him had promised. Of late, indeed, he had been quite unfriendly; had displayed a touch of meanness even, in shooting a fine colt of the doctor's that had broken out, and found a way into Joe's pasture.

"I ought to sue him and make him pay for it," said the physician, "and I would, only that I believe he is trying to provoke me into a quarrel."

Since the killing of the colt, that sense of littleness, the sure effect of a cowardly deed, had kept Joe at a distance. What had he done, the doctor wondered, to so arouse the animosity of the young fellow? If he had wronged him he was more than willing to make atonement, if he only knew wherein the wrong consisted.

He was soon to be enlightened; the enlightenment, or the bringer of it, was calling and signalling from the bluff above the roadside.

"Doctor Borin'," she called, "O Doctor Borin'! wait thar a minute if you please, Doctor Borin'; I am comin' down by the path to speak ter you-uns."

Nothing loath, he seated himself upon a great gray boulder at the foot of the bluff, and waited, while Mrs. Tucker ran down the path to meet him.

She stood before him at last, breathless, panting, and, although she made an effort to disguise it, he saw that she was excited.

"Doctor Borin'," she said, "I want ter have a settlemint with you-uns, for doctorin' of me whenst I ware took sick last month. I want a settlemint."

Accustomed to humanity in many phases, he saw at once that she was manœuvring.

"A settlement?" he replied. "Well,

bring me half a dozen chickens. I'm not going to skip the country yet, and I don't believe you are."

The worried expression in her face did not leave it, as she said, "Doctor Borin', you air a good man; you have been mighty clever ter me an' mine."

"Much obliged, madam," said the doctor, a twinkle in his eyes. But she gave no heed to the interruption.

"I wish you well, Doctor Borin'; I ud hate mightily if anything ware ter happen ter you-uns."

"Well," he said, "am I in any danger, Mrs. Tucker?"

The amusement left his face; an expression of annoyance came in its place.

"Yes, Doctor Borin', I'm afeard you air. Leastways — won't you take t'other path home? I ain't a-sayin' anybody ud be mean enough or sneak enough or coward enough ter hurt you unbeknownst. But I wish't you'd take the mount'n path home, 'stid o' the valley path."

Her solicitude touched him keenly. But there was no coward taint in his blood; the man who had braved creeds, religious and social ostracism, was not the man to quail before a physical danger. He hesitated, but only in order to shape his language into form not to wound her.

"Neither shall I," he said, "be small enough or weak enough or coward enough to turn my back to a hidden danger. Madam, no coward ever sees the old doctor's heels!"

"Then won't you go, t'other way I mean, for *me*? Jest ter pleasure an ole woman who air obligated ter yer, an' who wishes you well? Won't you do it — for *me*, Doctor Borin'?"

She laid her hard old hand upon his sleeve; in the faded eyes tears were starting; the thin lips twitched in a way that was almost painful to witness. Watching her, there stirred in his heart a feeling which had slumbered for years. Before him, between the yellow old face and his own, another face arose, his mother's; gentle, wistful, the tears in the sad, fathomless eyes, the white lips a-quiver with pain as they pleaded with him to forgive, to forget, for *her* sake. He had truly *tried* for *her* sake; for her sake he would "pleasure" this humble old woman who had come to him in his mother's stead.

"Well, well," he said, "if it will be any gratification to you I will take the path down the mountain and go home the back way. But you must know that I am not afraid of dangers that hide in the bush; because I am not afraid of death, perhaps; it is life that makes cowards of men, not death. I hope you are not going to ask me to put on your sunbonnet, madam."

He was laughing again, as he walked by her side, up the mountain to a point where her path met the path leading to his cabin.

"Naw, sir, I sha'n't ask you to do that," she replied; "but, Doctor Borin', if you meet Lissy Reams on the way, I wish't you wouldn't stop ter talk ter her."

He gathered himself together, looked her full in the eye, and said, "*Hell!*"

"I knowed that ware just what you would say. But I wish you would mind what *I* say. I'm goin' up this way now; I'll come down an' fetch the chickens to-morrer, maybe this evenin'; good-day, Doctor Borin'."

Her black sunbonnet appeared now and then, bobbing above the laurel where her path wound among the short stunted growth. He watched it a moment, the tail flapping in the breeze like the wings of a great crow about to alight among the bushes. Then he turned and went slowly down the mountain. He forgot the wrinkled old face under the sunbonnet's shade; to his vision appeared only the sublimity of gratitude, in an earnest, simple heart. She had tramped all that distance to warn him of a fancied, perhaps a possible, danger.

When she had eaten her dinner she caught six of her best young pullets, and, tying their legs securely with strips of old cotton, set off down the mountain again. All her fears were reawakened. She had seen Joe ride by with a rifle flung across the saddle-bow.

How he laughed at her, the odd, death-defying old doctor:

"Why, my good woman," said he, "I am no more afraid of Joe Bowen than I am of you. He will never shoot me, don't you believe it; not if I can get a word with him before he pulls the trigger. If he does he will have to shoot me in the back, and Joe Bowen isn't a coward, whatever may be his faults."

"He's crazy," she insisted. "He's ravin' mad, a-thinkin' as how you-uns air tryin' ter keep company with Lissy Reams. I told him myself that he was a fool, an' little better than a idiot, ter s'pose you ware thinkin' o' that chil'.

An' you ole enough ter be her gran'-father, a-mighty nigh."

He coloured, and dropped his eyes; the folly of his thought had been brought home to him many times during the day. Strange he had not seen it himself. Yet if he chose—that pure, wax-like nature—

He put the temptation aside; he would put a thorn in no man's content.

"You are very good to think of me," he said. "And Joe is very foolish to hold such ideas. Yes, I am an old man,—an old man. Old enough to be her father; yes, quite so, quite so."

He had forgotten her presence, and sat with his head dropped forward, and his eyes fixed upon the fire. The vibrant clearness of her voice, when she spoke again, quite startled him. "Can't we have a settlemint now, Doctor Borin'?"

He glanced up, quickly:

"Bring me another half dozen chickens," he said.

He sat there long after she had gone,

his head drooped upon his breast, his eyes fixed upon the glowing coal bed. The gold of the afternoon faded; the gray twilight set in, and then the night, starlit and cold. Ephraim came in and built up the fire, but the physician did not stir. At last old Dilce called him to supper, and he got up, exchanging without thought his coat for the purple dressing-gown.

As he stood before the mantel, he caught a glimpse of his face in the little mirror above it. His head had never looked so white, his eyes so wearily heavy. "Old enough to be her father," he murmured, resting a moment against the mantel.

"De supper am gittin' col', marster."

"Yes, yes, I am coming. I forgot all about it, I am afraid." Then, softly, "An old man; old enough to be her father; quite so, quite so."

Yet he remembered that she had said, "You don't appear to be so old."

Chapter X

JOE had not stopped in the valley, as Mrs. Tucker feared, to waylay Doctor Boring. The physician had judged him more correctly. Joe was not a coward; he would shoot him with half an excuse for doing so; he would go further, and create the opportunity; but he would not, except it be upon impulse, shoot from ambush.

Joe rode past the cabin in the valley without turning his head; he was riding the black, spirited colt he had lately purchased, alas! for Alicia, when Alicia should be his wife. The fact did not augment his good humour. He rode briskly by, sitting his mount like an Indian, down to Cowan, where he spent the day loafing, and nursing his wrath, among the usual

Saturday visitors "to town." Bowen was not a drinker; when he drank it was more as a frolic than a brunt to bad feeling, or a taste for alcohol.

He was not in a humour for fun, so he sat by, sullen and unhappy, listening to the gossip, political and social, until the dusky red of twilight sent the gossipers on their homeward way. Still he lingered, loath to return to his desolate hearth, shorn as it was of the bright dreams that had been his fireside friends of late.

It was past nine when he rode down the valley. Far before him he saw the round, red eye which he knew to be the doctor's window, through which the mingled glow of lamp and firelight streamed out upon the night and sent its good, glad glow far down the valley; a guide to the benighted, a promise to the wanderer pushing homeward through the darkness.

Something in its brightness appealed to Joe; there came to him a feeling that the world was not, after all, so desolately cheerless as he had fancied. He followed the tiny ray without realising it for a while; thinking, without realising it, just how good the warmth must be within that little valley home; how dark outside, and how cold. His horse's hoofs struck the frozen earth with a harshness that seemed to ring and vibrate. The contrast suddenly opened about and faced him,—their two lives, the difference of surroundings, the warmth within where *he* was, the blackness of night which accompanied *him*. Yet he did not care for these things; he was not so small as that. But that this man, with all the favour of fortune, with ease, comfort, everything,— that he should seek to rob him, *had* robbed him of the one single flower that had ever lifted its face to gladden the humble path where fate had set *him* down,—this was the sting, this was the injustice which rankled and burned and turned his natural goodness to hate.

"He ain't fittin' ter live," he muttered,

between his strong, set teeth. "He ain't fittin' ter be *let* live. If I ware ter aim a bullet square at that red pane o' winder, 'twould find his gray head straight as straight. An' it air no more than he deserves, a bullet ain't. But I ain't that low, I reckin, to shoot a man in the back. Naw, Lord! if I kill a bird I let it git the start. I'll be as gen'rous ter a man as I am ter a pa'tridge, though he ain't as deservin'."

He still carried his gun slung across the saddle-bow, and the red pane drew nearer, seemed to grow, to expand, until eighteen small square panes took shape, every pane aglow, and beyond them the doctor's large gray head, resting upon his hand, his elbow upon the table near which he sat reading.

The devil whispered in Joe's ear a dastardly thing; a thing too cowardly mean for the eye of God's good daylight. Only under cover of night could such a deed find birth. But it came so sharp and strong and sudden, was so irresistibly fascinating, so fiendishly fraught with the sweetness of revenge complete, that he had no time to meet the terrible temptation. He forgot his consideration for the "bird;" forgot his manhood, everything but the rank revenge that for the moment robbed him of his reason.

Quick as a flash he lifted the gun to his shoulder and took aim; his keen eye flashed along the muzzle for a single instant; his finger pressed the trigger, which refused to act; an instant yet, and the gray head was lifted; the calmly gentle face turned as though to catch a sound for which the ear had waited; then the figure vanished.

The next moment the door opened, and from it came a stream of crimson light that lay aslant the darkness like a path of fire. In the very centre of it stood the doctor, erect and fearless. What a target against the light, as he stood with his back to the door, his arms outspread, resting a hand on either casing! Joe uttered an oath, and dropped his gun with a sudden snap that brought the hammer of the old-fashioned weapon down upon his finger clumsily feeling for the cock. The noise of his horse's hoofs sounded in his ears like drums beating furiously. Suddenly the doctor put his hands to his mouth and hailed:

"O Joe! Bowen!" The only evidence that Joe heard was the sudden silence as the rider brought his horse to a standstill. The physician accepted the silence for attention. "Come by," said he. "Stop; I want to see you."

It was an instance of the incomprehensible power of will, the stronger over the weaker. The very attitude of the man standing there defying danger, the mere tone of voice, all had about it that which compelled obedience.

Joe hesitated an instant only, then wheeled his horse into the footpath leading to the doctor's gate.

The physician stood in the doorway while his visitor twisted his bridle into the iron ring dangling from the hitching-post, which few callers ever saw, the limbs of the trees being more familiar to the service. He came up the walk, gun in hand, his long, gaunt shadow growing longer and more gaunt with every step towards the light.

"Come in; walk right in there to the fire; you must be half frozen. Nobody there but Zip; Zip and I are making ourselves comfortable after our own ideas. Do likewise; do likewise. I will join you in just a minute."

Scarcely knowing what he did, and inwardly cursing himself for "a dad-blamed fool," Bowen obeyed. The room was tempting; the doctor himself was tempting; even the terrier curled up on the hair sofa looked up with an air which said, "Well, now, we *are* comfortable." There was a homefulness about it all that invited confidence.

In a moment the doctor returned. The first object to arrest his eye was the old flintlock rifle leaning against the wall; the next moment he saw the hand resting upon Joe's knee, with the blood slowly oozing from a wound in the right forefinger.

"Why, man," said the physician, "you have wounded yourself. Wheel about to the light and let us have a look at it. Sure it isn't another case of hornet sting?"

The guilty crimson swept the boyish face, turned for a moment to the lamplight. He had forgotten all about the wounded hand, so much sharper had been the hurt in the heart.

"I reckin it ain't much," he said, with sullen indifference, making an effort to conceal the bleeding member under the palm of the other.

"Oh, come now," said the doctor, "this will not do. Put it out here; that is what I am here for. You wouldn't cheat an old man out of his trade, would you? Give me your hand, boy."

He had been arranging a few simple implements while he talked, — a case of steels, a sheet of plaster, a roll of soft, starchless linen lay on the table.

Joe eyed him sullenly. Suddenly he rose; his tall, straight figure towered above the other like the figure of a young Goliath. His eyes flashed, and from the uplifted wounded finger drops of bright red blood trickled the length of his hand, disappearing under his sleeve.

"Damn you!" he hissed. "Say out what you've got to say; I ain't here to fool an' palaver with you-uns. I see you at that thar table when I rid up, an' I ware tempted to put a bullet into you. I had my gun aimed, cocked, when you moved off out of range. An' the damn thing snapped, ketchin' of my finger. That's how come the wound you're beggin' leave ter patch up. An' it ware me killed your horse, the fine colt. I done it to make sure you'd never saddle Lissy Reams on to hit, like you done on t'other one. An' it ware me — oh, damn it all! Git up from thar an' kick me out. Or else come outside an' fight it out like men fight. An' if you whip me you may take the gal an' go to the devil, an' I'll quit the country. But don't, in God A'mighty's name, set thar saaft-sawderin' o' me. I can't take it, an' I won't."

The doctor slowly rose; he was trembling. Afraid? For an instant Joe thought so. Only for an instant, however; until he saw the face of the man. There was no agitation in the calm eyes, although the hand which he rested upon the table to steady himself shook.

"The man who would fight with me," said he, in slow, even accents, " must content himself with a very one-sided battle. And the coward lying for my life like a thief outside my window, under cover of night and of darkness, will not find lack of opportunity for taking it. The day has never dawned that found me afraid to die. To the honest man, always, death is only a part of life's plan, and, let it come when and as it will, can neither alter nor affect that plan.

"To me life has never held an hour that found me unwilling to lay it down; seldom brought a gift so fair that I have sighed for its renunciation. Do you suppose that I am afraid of *you*? or *any* man? That I would have moved my head the fraction of an inch to dodge your coward-bullet? Do the old, you think, find life so full, its happiness so vast, that they hug it like a miser his gold? Sometimes, perhaps, but it is where ties are many and love has outlived years. Not so with me; I am an old man as compared with you: the fifty years that have slipped the measure in my glass were not so many grains of gold to dazzle and amuse, but so much of good life and strength stripped from the old shell called manhood. Sit down there. I want to tell you a story;

having told it, you know where your gun is; and the window will not be closed. Sit down, man; don't be a fool, if you can help it."

He forced him to the chair again, and again began to adjust his surgical instruments.

"Give me your hand; now, while I patch this hole up, all I ask of you is to listen. I have always refused to believe you a coward. It remains to be seen whether or not you are the fool your recent conduct would argue."

Accustomed to the sick, he had long ago learned to exact obedience of his patients. This man was as truly his patient as if he were suffering some acute disease of the body. And as such he treated him. The dark face lost something of its angry defiance, while the restless eyes furtively followed the deft fingers patting a bit of plaster upon the ugly pinch the rifle had made in the long forefinger. There was seductive sweetness in the voice that pronounced him "a fool," a something that soothed even while it condemned. Before the doctor had proceeded well into his story Joe began to suspect that he was right; that he *was* "a fool."

"I find," said the doctor, "that in order to get your thoughts at rest I must tell you a little story that concerns chiefly myself. I had hoped that it was buried for ever, or until the last resurrection of all pain. I am an old man at fifty, older than you will be at seventy. At twenty I left college; at twenty-two was a practising physician. That I made success of my profession, no one ever denied. Life held fair promises for me. I was not a Christian, as the world accepts the term. I denied many things, doubted more, that orthodoxy accepted. Mine is an open nature, and I saw no reason for concealment; so that everybody who knew me knew my creed, if I had one. That I have done some good the poor will bear witness at the last. If I have harmed any man I do not know it. I made myself a place and practice. At last there came into my life a being who changed its current; awoke the heart within me; played upon its every string; sounded every depth, knew every shallow, of my nature. It was at the bedside of her dying father that we first met; we became lovers, plighted our troth, were soon to have been married. She was poor; I had plenty. That she was influenced by my wealth was a thought too insulting to have lodging in the same heart that held her. If I found her lacking in demonstration of affection, I attributed it to maiden modesty and was content. She was a Christian, after the favoured order. There was in her family a cousin, a reckless young fellow, who hung about her some, but of whom I had as little jealousy as I have, or might have, of my terrier asleep there on my couch.

"My wedding-day was fixed; was near; but two days gaped between my happiness and me. My best man was an old college chum whom I had lifted out of debt, saved from disgrace once, and given many a turn along the way. The day before that fixed for my marriage I met him, but when I would have greeted him he turned his face away. Was he angry, drunk? I crossed the street and faced him; he was laughing. He looked so guilty, Bowen, so vulgarly guilty, that with my left I grasped my right hand in order not to strike him down. It was only for an instant, however; in a twinkling he was himself again. But for the life of me I couldn't rest. I felt that I had done my friend injustice. I sought him out again before the day was done, and made my full apology. Then, 'Jack,' said I, 'go down and select my ties for me. You've got good taste about such things.'

"'Oh, let the ties be, Doc,' was his reply; 'there's time enough. I'll see to them, old boy, — *in time.*'

"That night I called on Alice. I never saw her half so radiant, so superbly lovely. I was all happiness; one thing only came between my joy and me. She refused my good-night kiss. I left her early: she wanted her 'beauty sleep,' she said. And since it was her last day of girlhood I resigned her to herself, knowing it *was* the last time. When I reached my room I read a chapter from a little velvet Bible, her gift, which, to please her, I had promised to read daily.

"The following morning I went early to my office; the few acquaintances I met upon the street dodged me,—unmistakably dodged me.

"As I was passing the house of a man who had been my father's friend and as stanchly mine, I saw him open the door and come down the walk to the gate. I said good-morning from across the street, and would have passed on, but that he called me:

"'Come in,' said he. 'I wish to see

you; have been watching at the window for you.'

"I crossed over and went in. I remember that the sun shone, and that there were scarlet gladiolus blooming in the window, although it was bitter cold.

"He led me in, motioned to a chair, himself took one, and then I saw his face. Some dreadful thing had happened. I waited for him to go on.

"'Bart,' said he, 'I had rather cut my tongue out than to tell you—'

"'Is something wrong?' said I. 'Tell me; let me help you if I can.'

"He motioned me to silence. 'The trouble,' said he, 'is not mine, but yours.'

"'Mine?'

"'Brace yourself to hear it,' said he. 'It isn't a sweet duty to dash a man's happiness to death, to crush both pride and joy at a blow.'

"He was sparring, as he thought, mercifully. But I cut him off. 'Tell me,' said I; 'I'm not a child. What is it that has happened?'

"It was Alice; she had run away the night before, eloped, and been married to her cousin.

"Bowen, it struck me like an iron hammer. My head dropped on my breast like lead; my heart, that had held warm blood, turned to ice while I listened to the story of her falseness, my shame, and my betrayal by my friend; for Jack was one of the attendants and witnesses; had helped her to elude me; gone with her upon her midnight visit to a little village clergyman, who had married the runaways. I heard it all, the shameful, cruel story, and then I roused myself to meet my fate, scarcely harder to encounter than the smiles or the unspoken sympathy, as it chanced, from those who saw the humour or the pathos of the situation. There was one who saw the *tragedy*,— my mother,— and it killed her.

"I heard the story through and then I lifted my head.

"'It's pretty hard,' I said, 'but I think that I can bear it.'

"He grasped my hand, pressed it, and burst into tears.

"I went to my room with head erect; I greeted my friends along the way. They looked at me as if they thought me mad.

"Opening my door, the first thing met my eye was the little velvet Bible, open where I had read the night before. I took it in my hand, glanced down at the open page where she had traced a text, — '*And the truth shall make you free,*' — and tossed it in the fire. I have never opened one since then, not from that day to this. I got into my buggy, visited my patients all day, at night went home, stealing in softly so that my mother need not be disturbed. But she was waiting; had waited for me all the day. She saw my face and read my heart. The smile, the quiet, matter-of-fact manner that had bewildered my friends were not needed here. She put her arms around my neck and fainted. She alone knew how one woman's perfidy had made shipwreck of a strong man's tottering faith. Trouble comes in battalions: I buried my mother in less than a year. I lived on there, though friends urged me, having my own comfort at heart, to go elsewhere; every feeling in my nature rebelled against cowardly flight. I remained until I proved myself equal to my destiny.

"It is almost thirty years since I passed down the steps of my friend's house that crisp, cold morning, and went out to face ridicule, and the pity that was scarcely less difficult to bear. I remember that the sun shone, and that the scarlet gladiolus were frozen stiff against the window-pane. They looked like spots of clotted blood against the frosted glass. I thought of them when I saw your wounded hand to-night.

"Come: you have my story; the true heart has but its *one*, ever."

The clock above the mantel monotonously ticked off the time; the wounded hand, sponged and bound, lay on the doctor's knee; the strong, clear profile of the guest shone with cameo effect against the crimson firelight as the owner turned his face from the physician's. Suddenly he faced him; in the clear depths of his eyes, lately so defiant, the tears shone like drops of crystal.

"And you didn't *kill* him?" he said,—"you didn't kill him like you would kill a dog?"

"No, he lives yet; she is dead, though, years ago."

"You ought ter 'a' killed him. He ware not fittin' to live."

"Would his death have restored to me that which her untruth had lost me,—my peace, my faith, my mother?"

"Well, no," said Joe, "but I'd 'a' killed him. I'd 'a' had my satisfaction that far."

"No," said the doctor; "I chose the better part, I hope. Love isn't quite *all* of life; though it is so nearly all that we sometimes make the mistake of thinking it quite so. That is, we who feel intensely. For me, I gathered my burden to my shoulders as best I could, and for thirty years almost I have stumbled along with it in the dark. In the dark! Ah, that is the hardest part of pain: that he who bears her company must, at the starting, turn his back upon the light. So I have travelled with her all these weary years, in the dark. But, Bowen,—"

He leaned forward, placing a hand upon either knee of his visitor, compelling his strict attention,—"I resolved, with God's help and man's strength, that I would never be the despoiler of any man's happiness. That is why I called you in to-night."

He got up hastily, and began to walk the floor. Joe regarded him steadily a moment; then he, too, arose. His strong young face bore index to the brave young heart beneath it; shame, sympathy, regret, and the courage of acknowledgment, all were visible in the bold, brown features lifted to the light.

"Doctor Borin'," he said, "I have been a fool; I have been a great fool. I'd like to ask yo' — "

"It was granted long ago," said the doctor. "Look at the clock, — twelve. That is your candle on the mantel. Aunt Dilce built your fire two hours ago."

The mountaineer regarded him stupidly; he had a faint suspicion that the rehearsal of his wrongs had unsettled the man's mind.

"If Zip don't min' lettin' me have that hat o' mine he's made his bed in, I'm goin' home," said Joe. "I reckin my nag is in an' about froze by this time."

"Your horse has been in the stable for hours; ever since you came. You are not going away from here to-night. The guest-chamber is waiting for you. We are to be friends from this on, Joe. We will begin by your sharing my roof to-night."

He was lighting the candle as he spoke; when he held it to the mountaineer the latter shook his head.

"Not yet," said he. Then, with sudden vehemence, "I tell you, Doctor Borin', I ain't fittin' ter be yo' friend. I want ter be, but, O Lord!—I tell you I ain't fittin'. First, you must take my horse for the one I killed."

"We will talk about that to-morrow," said the doctor.

"No, sir, to-night, *now*. You must promise to take my horse; he's a good one, an' I'm fond of him. But I'll feel like a thief, an' a sneak-thief at that, unless you say you'll take him. He's in your stable, thar he stays, an' we're even. Be it so?"

"Be it so," said the doctor.

"Good; gimme my light; though I ain't sayin' as I don't feel like a blamed fool, an' a horse thief, an' Brother Barry, all at once."

He thundered up the stair, spilling the hot sperm upon the linen bandage that enwrapped his wounded hand. The physician sat a long while before the fire, his head dropped forward in the weary way that had come to him of late.

"A disturber of no man's peace," he said, softly, as he bent to lay a shovelful of ashes on the dying coals. "A spoiler of no man's happiness. No man can charge me with that. Yet I could have won her, — she is very gentle, and pliable, and sympathetic; I could have — won." The white ashes grew cold, shifted, and fell apart while he sat there, head bowed, hands folded, lost in thought. When the clock upon the mantel struck three he started, rose, and shook himself. "And now," said he, "there is nothing left but to turn down the page." Alas! turning down the page does not always ensure forgetting.

He turned off his lamp and crept into bed. The moonlight through the window where he had failed to drop the curtain fell upon his face while he slept; gently, a caress in each silvery beam, as if they would have smoothed the lines that grief had traced upon his brow, and comforted him.

When he awoke the sun shone, and his guest was gone.

"Tromped off befo' breakfus," said Ephraim, "leavin' his black horse in de stable."

The presence of the horse confirmed the presence of his master, which in the good light of day the doctor was for an instant disposed to regard as a part of the night's dreams; it gave the stamp of genuineness to Joe's regret for past unfriendliness.

Later in the day Lissy stopped at the gate to ask the doctor to go up and see Lucy Ann's baby.

"It's real bad off," she declared, "with the measles."

It was such a message as she brought any day, yet she was awkward and slow in delivering it, and he noticed that the gray eyes refused to meet his with their old-time frankness.

Joe's jealousy had revealed the physician in a new light; the mere suspicion of love had poisoned the perfect friendship.

"Are you going back up there?" said the doctor.

"I can go if you want to send somethin'," she replied, "but I'll have to hurry back home again." It was the first time since he had known her that she had not found time to devote to the sick.

"No," he said, "I can go up, though I am a little busy. It is a tiresome walk, and you have taken it once this morning. Moreover, you seem to be as busy as I."

Without a moment's hesitation, she stepped into the trap he set for her.

"It ain't anything but can wait as well

as not," she insisted. "An' I don't mind the walk a bit. I'm strong an' young. You better send me in yo' stead."

She had not meant to hurt him, he knew it. He knew that to her the years that lay between them were as nothing. Yet her words hurt. He began to see how old he must appear to other people; began to see himself that he was an old man; "an old fool," he said, "so old that even Joe Bowen had comprehended at last the folly of being jealous of such an ancient." But there he did himself and Joe injustice. That gentleman had never discovered any reason on earth why the doctor should not love and marry Alicia, save that he wanted her for himself. Joe's was a primitive faith. To his thinking, love could come but once. And this love of the doctor's, with its tincture of tragedy, must, according to his idea, for ever disbar the heart where it had been harboured against all meaner passions. That first love is all-love is not always granted by those more worldly wise than Joe. But with him it was not a question of will; he had failed to catch the finer point of honour with which the physician meant to pledge himself, in an unspoken promise, not to interfere with his love affair. To him it was simply an impossibility; as much so as the new growth of a limb that has been amputated from the human body. With him love had no second birth. A primitive faith, and, like other primitive beliefs, gone to find a grave in the cobwebbed past.

Alicia refused to "come in," but said "good-mornin'" in the stiffest way, and went home.

"Anybody would think, to see her," mused the doctor, "that I had robbed her hen-roost, or refused to pay my truck bill."

The coming of Mrs. Tucker, a few minutes later, changed the current of his thought:

"Doctor Borin'," she began, "I reckin I pester you a heap with my troubles. I reckin we *all* pester you, right smart."

"Sit down there by the fire," said the doctor, "and while you are thawing tell me what the 'trouble' is this time. What is a physician for, if not to listen to the ailings of his patients?"

She took the chair he placed for her, and, pushing back the familiar black bonnet, said:

"Doctor Borin', I have come down here to ax you for a settlemint. I reckin the interest on my debt to you will in an' about eat me out o' house an' home. You air a town doctor, but a mighty good one. I ain't faultin' of you for bein' a town man; you couldn't holp that. But I have heard say town men axed mighty high for theirse'ves, an' I'm a po' woman. But I'm honest; an' you'll git yo' pay, Doctor Borin', if I have to sell my house an' bit o' lan' for it. I've come down here to tell you so, an' ter ax for a settlemint."

"Haven't time to-day," laughed the doctor. "Besides, I have a new patient at your house. Wait until I cure the baby, then we'll bunch the debts and make one of them. I want you to take some medicine up to Lucy Ann; and see that the measles don't 'go in,' and that the baby doesn't take cold. No, it isn't any use to try to pin me down to arithmetic to-day. I am going down to Pelham to call on Joe Bowen; he promised to let me have a load of hay for my horse."

He saw the worried expression come into her eyes, and gave up teasing.

"Wait," he said. "How much do I owe you?"

She was an honest trader, a careful accountant.

"You owe me," she replied, in a slow, businesslike way, "two dollars an' seventy-five cents. I owe you — "

"I am keeping my side of the account," he interrupted her to say. "You look to yours."

"I am gittin' to be an ol' woman, Doctor Borin'," she continued, "an' I want to leave myse'f square with the world when I come ter quit it. I owe you so much that I've been a'most afeard ter ax you how much it air. But I've saved up a little money ter he'p pay you, anyhow, an' I'm proper glad to git you ter talk about it at last. That two dollars an' seventy-five cents—"

"There it is," said the doctor. "I am putting it into your egg basket, since you do not seem to see it. And now, my good woman, we are *square*. That is our settlement."

She stared first at him, then at the silver he had slipped into her basket.

"But, Doctor Borin'," she began, when he again interrupted her:

"Bring me some more chickens; if I haven't emptied your roost."

She understood at last, and went out, silent, the tears in her eyes and in her throat, choking her.

The next morning Lissy came down to the gate and sent for him to come out. Al was sick; he had been taken with a chill the night before, and she had wished to come for him then, but her grandmother was opposed to it. She had given him a quantity of pepper tea and had put him to bed, to wait for the herb doctor.

"He's real sick, Doctor Borin'," Alicia continued, "an' I wish you would go over an' see him befo' the herb doctor gets there."

"I cannot do that, Lissy," he replied; "but if you will come in I will fill some quinine capsules for Al. But you must come in the house. I shall not touch them if you insist upon hanging on my gate-post for half an hour in the cold."

She hesitated, blushing. It did not appear altogether proper for her to go in alone, and no woman there but an old negress. While she hesitated he opened the gate and led her in, up the walk, into the little sitting-room where patients and other visitors came every day, almost every hour of the day.

"What in the name of common sense has come over you, child?" he asked, fretfully, in order to disguise the pleasure he felt in having her once more sitting opposite him at his own hearth. "You're getting tired of the old hospital, Lissy; I just know that's it. And everybody else in the neighbourhood likes it, likes to come here. Mrs. Tucker sat an hour, only yesterday."

His words and manner quite reassured her. After all, she was fond of coming over and chatting with him before the big fire, with the terrier asleep in her lap, and Aunt Dilcy putting her head in now and then to give the milk jar a turn on the hearth where she always set it until ready for the churn. Sometimes Al came over with her, and then the visit was real pleasant. But of late,—well, after all, she failed to detect any difference in the doctor's manner; so she concluded Joe had allowed his jealousy to warp his good sense. The doctor didn't appear near so fond of her as he did of the terrier on her lap.

"I will fill the capsules," he said, seating himself to the task, "and you may give one to Al every two hours. You can give them on the sly if there's any fuss made."

"I'll give them fair an' square, if granny'll let me," she replied. "I won't do anything on the sly. I reckin granny'll throw it all in the fire for a lot o' foolishness, because it's bitter instead of hot. Granny believes in fire. Grandad says that's why she's so wedded to the bad place; it's hot. He says hell's about the only medicine ever give that was hot enough for granny. An' he says she's equal to a pretty big dose of that. Doctor Borin', if I ever get sick I want *you* to doctor me. Remember now, you're notified befo'hand. Will you?"

"If you let me know you are ill before you send for the undertaker," he replied, tapping the quinine bottle with his finger until the white fluffy powder lay in a soft heap on the paper he had spread upon the table to receive it. "You people have a way of getting sick and sending for a physician while they are taking your measure for a coffin."

She laughed softly, twirling her hat upon her slender, well-shaped finger.

"Well, I'm too healthy to send for either of you *yet*," she said. "When I die — " She glanced up, caught the expression in his eyes, and blushed. Was Joe right after all? His next words almost made her think herself a fool.

"Be sure you are not guilty of such a thing until I get home again," said he. "I am going back to the city soon, to be gone — months."

He was watching her now, so intently she dared not look up, and so failed to read the truth, as Joe had seen it, in his eyes. He saw her start, however, and his heart gave a sudden joyous bound, although she went on talking quietly, even merrily, of his going.

"I sha'n't die befo' you get back, I reckin. I'm healthy an' strong. I reckin I ought to be thankful; I *am* thankful, though I ain't as rejoiced over the comin' back of Brother Barry as I might be."

He was silent, hoping she would talk on; it was a happiness to have her sit there in his house, and prattle in her sweet, girlish way. But when she drew her chair a trifle nearer the table, and began helping him to fill the capsules in a matter-of-fact, at-home way, his happiness was complete, so thoroughly in her proper place did she appear. "I reckin," she went on to say, "they're all expectin' a big revival. Joe said he lay I'd give in this time sure. An little Al has asked granny ter ask the church folks to pray for him. I know he's a sight better than a lot of them, but I don't say so; I wouldn't hinder nobody, let alone little Al. But for me, I can't see my way plain to believe. They haven't explained away that resurrection of the body yet; not to *my* satisfaction."

He could help her over this stone at all events.

"Lissy," he said, "that is the easiest part of the problem. Listen, — "

He leaned forward, a half-filled capsule in his hand, his arm resting upon the table.

"You put a seed in the ground in the spring-time, — a grain of corn. In a little while there appears a tender shoot of green, and you say your seed has 'come up;' yet it is not a seed; it is no longer a grain of corn. And if you dig there the next spring, and every spring until decay has carried it away, you will find the rotted roots, the skeleton of the seed you sowed. Yet the seed came up, albeit in another form. *Was* it the seed you sowed? So it is with our natural body; it is sown in corruption, in the earth; it is raised a spiritual body, incorruptible. Like the seed you sow, it is not the body which shall be, but bare grain, 'it may chance of wheat, or of some other grain.' But 'God giveth it a body,' a new body, just as He gives a new form to your seed when you say it has come up."

She had listened with a kind of rapt intentness while he unravelled the mystery of her doubt. When he finished, a smile parted her lips. "Why, it's as easy as anything!" she laughed. "I see it as plain as day now. Doctor Borin', I wonder if the rest might not be just as easy, with somebody to explain it all?"

"Just as easy, dear — child," he replied, blushing like a boy for the slip his tongue had made. "Just you go on living one day at a time, doing your duty as seems right to you, and letting creeds and mysteries take care of themselves.

Take this for your creed, 'For me, I do believe in God and love.' That's creed enough to live by, and life well lived will light death's lantern; never doubt it."

The gray eyes were aglow with surprised delight.

"Why, Doctor Borin', you're not an infidel!" she said. "You talk like the preacher."

"*What?*"

She laughed aloud. "I mean the Episcoper, at Sewanee, not Brother Barry. O Lord! I hope you don't think I'd call you like Brother Barry. But you ain't like an infidel, neither."

"Joe says I am."

"Oh, Joe; he's always talkin'; and he certainly does talk scan'lous sometimes; but it's funny, too; to save my life I can't help laughin' at him sometimes. Joe says that Moses left off one comman'ment he ought to have put down on them tables of stone. He forgot it, Joe says. '*Plough your own row.*' That's the other comman'ment Joe says as ought to have been put down. And he says he ain't been so mighty admirin' of them Israelites, who borrowed all their neighbours' earrings and jewelry, and then set out for the promised land. Joe says if they ware to try that these times all the promised land they'd reach would be the State prison. And he says just ordinary folks air runnin' this country, too, and not Moseses. That's what Joe says. Brother Barry says Joe's awful wicked, and something'll certain'y happen to him for his wickedness. Goodness knows I hope it won't be another cow to die with the milksick poison. I'm afraid Joe's sins will in and about kill up all his stock and cattle befo' I go down to Pelham. And when the two of us gets there I reckin both our sins, Joe's and mine, will about finish up things,— burn up the house, or set rust in the wheat or somethin'. Joe ought to think about that befo' he fetches another sinner to his farm. Good-by, Doctor

Borin'. I've got to carry the quinine to Al. It's mighty good of you to fix it for him. And I'm much obliged to you till you're better paid. You better come to meet'n' next month and get religion. Somethin' will happen to *you*, first thing you know. Zip might ketch the mumps, or somethin' else dreadful. You better stay here and get religion under Brother Barry, 'stead of runnin' off to town so soon."

Was she acting? More than once he had detected, or thought he had, an insincere note in her voice, and when she set him laughing over Joe's foolish sayings, he had looked up, to find that her own face was entirely destitute of mirth. He had been so satisfied to have her sit there in his house, at his side, so near him that her slight fingers among his capsules and powders touched his own more than once, thrilling him with strangely sweet content, that he had forgotten to sound her heart as he had meant to do, and to administer the advice for which indeed he had called her in.

"Lissy," he said, "sit still a moment. I want to talk to you."

She paled and flushed by turns, and nervously fingered the box of quinine with which he had provided her.

"Alicia," said the doctor, "have you and Joe adjusted your difference? I mean have you made up your quarrel?"

"No, sir," she replied; "we ain't friends; not like we useter be."

"Why?"

He saw the colour in her face deepen; her eyes were bent upon her hands, working nervously in her lap. Did he know? she wondered; did he think that she was fool enough to suppose that he could care for her,—a humble little peddler of the vegetables her own hands had raised? Embarrassment sealed her lips.

For him, he would have sounded her heart for the one certain blessed knowledge that he was not altogether merely a foolish old man to her.

He leaned forward to look into her eyes.

"Alicia," he said, the tenderness of his tone giving new music to the pretty, old-fashioned name. "Alicia, may I help you to set Joe right? I am an old friend, you know."

She flashed upon him with sudden vehemence:

"No, sir," she said; "I don't want any help to do that. But," she added, more gently, "I'm much obliged to you, Doctor Borin'. I know you mean it kind, but I haven't settled it in my own min' yet that I want to make it up with Joe."

"What?"

"I allowed you'd be surprised some; but Joe's been mighty foolish."

He flushed, understanding thoroughly wherein Joe's folly lay:

"How has he been 'foolish?' What has he done?"

He was watching her keenly; she was too honest, too innocently naïve not to betray her real feeling under his cunning probing.

"Well, he's been unreas'nable anyhow," she replied. "An' he has been mighty free with his fault-findin'. He has showed me somethin' in his disposition that I don't like, Doctor Borin'."

"Young men, young lovers, are always exacting, Alicia."

"Then I don't want 'em," she replied, with blunt honesty. "I won't have my life made a tirade and a continual jow. I aim to do some good in the worl' if I can; and if I marry at all, I'm going to marry a man steady and sober, an' live quiet and helpful. I ain't so mighty anxious to marry at all."

Again life offered him a chance; and again he chose the nobler part,— the nobler is ever the harder part.

"Alicia," he said, "you are young. But there is a womanliness about you that should win you a strong man's earnest love—"

He paused; she was looking straight into his eyes; as he continued he saw a warm light kindle in the shadowy gray depths of her own; a response that was ready to awaken with the slightest hint.

He leaned forward and folded her hands, palm to palm, between his own.

"You might have the life your heart calls for, the 'quiet, steady life.' And perhaps you would be content with it. But, dear — my dear child, it would slay your youth at the outset; drop you from girl to woman. And your content would consist in ignorance, since you would never know the real joy, the aliveness of happiness which only the young and sentimental may feel. You must live your youth, have your joy. Joe loves you, and his is an honest, earnest nature. He will never be unkind to you. The little whims of the lover do not appear in the husband. You must think of it, Alicia. I am going away soon, to be gone until the azaleas come again. When I return I shall expect to find you happy through my advice. You will not disappoint me,

Alicia? I am an old man, but in my youth, I, too, had a love; a love for a woman who cruelly cast it from her. And I can swear to you that an honest man's honest love doesn't easily die. Be good to Joe; a cruel woman is God's abomination; I feel sure of it. Go home now, and give Al his quinine. I have kept you a long time."

She rose with him, and he opened the door for her to pass out. Had she grasped his meaning? Had he hurt her? Her face, as he caught a last glimpse of it, wore a puzzled look; into the gray eyes the shadows had returned. His heart smote him sharply; but it was best, "best all round," he told himself; and that she "would soon forget it." As she reached the outer door, he called to her, pleasantly:

"Oh, Lissy, I am going to bring you a wedding present when I come back."

She waved her hand lightly, but gave him no other reply. Yet he noticed that, in the poise of her head, which he had never observed before. There was a dignity, almost a defiance, in the way she carried herself; her very feet seemed to touch the ground with new meaning; as though she demanded of the solid earth the strength of adamant, far down among its basic foundations.

The physician watched until the red-crowned head disappeared down the brown footpath.

"More strength than stability," was his thought. "Under favourable circumstances she would have developed a tendency to fanaticism. With a guiding hand, what a force she might prove in her day! As it is — ah, well; there is no telling the by-paths into which a nature like hers may turn."

Chapter XI

DOCTOR BORING had begun to feel at home in his cabin, and to find in the valley that content which life offers those who follow her humble leadings. In every work so much goes for charity; "for nothing," the world is accustomed to say of that for which no actual return in dollars is to be expected.

The physician, more than any man, if he be the true physician, gives more of himself to the poor than does any other man. Yet, does he stop to cast up the discount, — so much money, so many hours of sleep, so many miles of cold and sleet and suffering, so much hunger, so much time, so much of man's strength and vitality gone for nothing? Not he; he doesn't so much as consider "done for God's poor." He accepts it as a part of the price of success, as a duty done in the name of humanity, as so much of the discount demanded of his profession. But he responds to the calls. He who does not is a speculator in human suffering and unworthy the name of physician.

Doctor Boring had not put out his doorplate with any hope or wish for patients; it was merely a part of the whim that had bought the cabin and transferred him to the quiet valley paths. The little practice that he did was his "discount," his donation, in the name of his profession to humanity.

As the days grew colder he realised that if he meant to return to the city he must be off. Sometimes he was tempted not to go at all, — he was comfortable, content; what more had any man? But since his talk with Joe, and the promise made himself not to disturb the young man's happiness, he had decided to return at once,— in two days, perhaps.

He believed there was real good in young Bowen; for himself, he said, with a sigh, the path would soon reach the river, and he fancied the crossing would be clearer for the sacrifice made. Then, too, — and he tried to laugh at the recollection, — Bowen's first call had been his introduction to the people round about. It had set him in the balance, — learning against ignorance, skill against herbs. And he had felt his end of the scale go up until, he told himself, he had "kicked the beam like a trounced frog."

Yet this first call had been a godsend to him; had lifted him out of himself; inspired him with a determination to prove himself to those aristocrats of the wilderness; given him an entrance into their homes, a part and place in their lives. It had drawn him out from the shadows that dwarfed and the doubts that had upset his life; from the dogmas and creeds, whose "I believes" he had refused, and had, in consequence, found the great doors of Christianity closed upon him. So he had knocked at the doors of these native independents, who measure *men*, not their phylacteries. They had called to him that the latch-string hung upon the outside, with the same cordial good faith with which they responded to each other's knock, or to the knock of the parson himself,—that embodiment of all perfection. And since they had found him neither thief nor liar, they still accepted him as honest, even in his doubts, and granted him the privilege of believing "according to his light."

True, they still called him infidel, and believed that he would eventually be lost, burned in a lake of fire and brimstone; but with the same breath declared "'twould be a burnin' shame;" and sighed, unconscious they were guilty of a witticism.

To those he had left in the world he

had forsaken, there was a touch of tragedy in his life. They were a trifle disposed to call him the "mad doctor" also. Not because of the old romance to which he had refused to accord the privilege of ruining his life, — he had "outlived that," they said of him, "long enough before he left the world." Neither was it for the touch of heresy they pitied him; it was the voluntary giving up of the pleasures of society, those things for which his wealth and station fitted him, — his "self-immolation" they called it, — but they had ceased to believe that he would "soon grow weary of the wilderness." Nor would he. To him the hut in the valley was nearer the heaven his fancy painted and his heart called for, than any home he had found elsewhere; here he was not a cynic, not a scoffer, not a disturber of other men's content. No, no; no man could charge him with the despoiling of his happiness. The knowledge brought him infinite content. The happiness that had been denied his own life he had given another. It is a grand thing to give joy to a troubled heart; a glorious thing to scatter the rose seed along the barren wastes of a life, a blessed thing; the winds passing over the spot some day, and finding the roses abloom, will bring back their perfume, like sweet incense, to the nostrils of the sower.

With the cold came Brother Barry. Al, who had been but poorly all the fall, had at last taken to his bed with a chill. The old grandmother still refused the mad doctor's medicines, and poor Al had been at the mercy of herbs and hot teas.

The day following Alicia's visit Doctor Boring walked down the path to the miller's gate to inquire after the sick boy. It was early; he had not breakfasted, and the frost still lay white and glistening upon the short dry grass, and ridged the crisp brown stalks of the naked sumach and elder bushes.

The miller had lately met with reverses.

A visitor had dropped a spark from his pipe, and that night the mill had burned. The doctor missed the noisily monotonous clatter as he drew near the house, and stood a moment leaning upon the low gate, looking over into the shivering grays and browns that had lately been Alicia's truck-patch.

The doors of the house stood wide open, and beneath the window a denuded, frozen rose-bush tapped persistently against the pane.

A neighbour woman was spreading some quilts to air upon the ancient althea-bushes in the yard, the bright greens and yellows making a gaudy robing for the winter-stripped shrubs. On the door-step, her face buried in her folded arms, sat Alicia. The sun caught and duplicated the golden glints of her bright hair, as though rejoicing in the warmth of colour.

It was a pretty picture, despite the trouble in the background. He leaned over the gate and called:

"Lissy!"

The figure upon the doorstep did not stir.

"Lissy! Oh, Lissy! how is your brother?"

Still there was no response, and he called again:

"Lissy! O-h, *Lissy!* How is your brother?"

A neighbour woman came to the door, saw him, and said something in a low tone to the girl, seemingly deaf to his call. She lifted her head wearily, saw him, and placed her hand behind her ear; the wind was blowing contrary.

"How is your brother? Your brother? How — is — your — *brother?*"

The bright head fell back upon the folded arms. The neighbour woman shouted a reply, in a shrill, sharp voice, meant only to be distinct, however.

"What? Your brother is dead? *Hell!*"

He turned abruptly and went back to

his cabin, surprise, anger, disgust struggling within him. "These people!" he muttered; "they sit still and let one another die like pigs in a pen. Dosed on hot tea and set to cool in a draught that would make a bear sneeze. It's enough to make a man swear. A foot-bath and a few grains of quinine would have set that boy on his feet in three days. And here he is, *dead*. I declare I've a good mind to pull up stakes and quit the country."

As he approached his house he heard Aunt Dilce calling to Ephraim to "shut de front gate," and, looking up, for the first time discovered that he had a visitor.

The lank-looking mare industriously skinning the bark from a young sugar-tree proclaimed the ecclesiastical presence before old Dilce hobbled to the gate to announce the guest.

"De preacher ob de gospil, marster. An' lookin' lack he might be tolerable hongry fur his breakfus'."

He was grieved, troubled; yet he never permitted his own worries to affect his household, so he replied, as carelessly as possible, although he felt but little disposed for the company thrust upon him:

"Well, you must fix him up a good one. And tell Ephraim to take his mare and feed her, also."

The old negress's face wore a knowing look.

"He say he can't stay but just a minute; he say he got to git about de Marster's bus'nes."

He made a lunge at her with a stick he had cut from a sumach bush down the valley.

"Get out with you! as if you didn't know what Brother Barry's minutes mean. You old sinner!—go get the parson a good breakfast; fry another chicken, and make an extra pan of biscuit. Fill up your coffee-pot, and put fresh sheets on the bed in the garret. There's a revival to begin at Goshen, the big church down the valley. And the Master's business will locate Brother Barry in the guest-chamber for a week, at the very shortest. Go along, you old sinner, and help entertain the elect."

She went off, laughing and protesting; she understood the situation as well as he.

"Marster," she paused to say, "dey's plenty breakfus' done cooked fur half a dozen hearty eaters, en I ain' guine tech nare 'nother chicken; not fur nobody. It's ready en waitin'. You Efrum? come 'long here en tak dat mar' nag from dat sugar-tree, 'fo' I bus' it wide op'n."

The preacher was standing before the fireplace in the attitude of warming himself.

He turned to meet the doctor, in the old empty, high-sounding way. His voice had lost nothing of its drawling religious accent since his previous visit; his face wore its usual solemn aspect; he was, if possible, more dismally lachrymose than he had ever been. The sins of his people were more crushing than ever. He offered his hand cordially, in brotherly clasp, but without lifting his eyes.

"My brother," he said, in his solemn way, "the Master has sent me to you."

"Much obliged for the compliment," said the doctor, dryly. "But as I told you once before, I thought it was only to the lost sheep of the house of Israel you were sent. By the way, one of the flock has just died in the next house. Al Reams, the brother of Alicia, died an hour ago. You might be of service up there, instead of wasting ammunition on an old stray like me."

The face of the visitor wore a pious frown. Suddenly he lifted his hand and pronounced the doom of the dead boy:

"Died in his sins! died in his sins an' gone to hell. A warning! a warning! A theme for the evening service! — the death of the unregenerate; the soul that sinneth it shall surely die."

The sumach stick slipped from the

doctor's hand to the floor; he was all atremble with indignation.

"Do you mean to tell me that you expect to hold that dead boy up, a terror by which to drag your ignorant hearers out of hell fire? That boy, who never had an ugly thought in all his poor little life, and whose worst sin was an ignorant fear that somewhere, sometime, there might be reserved for him a punishment for the sins of which he had never so much as heard? The only brother and the idol of a broken-hearted sister who sits yonder crushed and broken with her loss, and whose only comfort is that the poor boy is happy with his God? And you would destroy that hope? assume the responsibility of the overthrow of that faith? *You? you?*"

"Let the living be warned by the dead," said the enthusiast. "Let them flee the wrath to come, lest they, too, be overtaken in their sins. The girl herself is a sinner; time an' again has the truth been presented, the offer refused. And now, for her stubbornness, the Lord has visited her with His rod. Let her be warned; let her be warned! Oh, I shall not preach the unregenerate into heaven: *I* have the courage to say he's in hell and the lake prepared for the devil an' his angels."

The doctor gave him a glance of intense scorn.

"Rot; nothing but rot. In less than ten years the man who gets up to cram such doctrine as that down the throat of an audience will find himself laughed out of the pulpit. Do you believe all that horrible stuff you're talking? If that is the kind of God you preach, then He is a fiend, and not a God. Stuff and nonsense! Go up there and help the poor people to live, if you can; ease their burden, not seek to crush them under it. Don't go straining at the gnat and swallowing the menagerie; and don't stand off and cry, 'The Lord, He did it!' I tell you He didn't. God doesn't strike in the back. Go up and tell the mourners in that cabin that He cares for them; that He has not smitten them; that He is not narrow and cruel and revengeful; that He established certain laws of health, and that one of these has been violated, and that is all. Tell them that hot teas and cold draughts killed their son and brother; not God; and that a dose of quinine taken in season would have accomplished that which that poor girl's prayers failed to do. Go up like a man, and a missionary indeed, and tell them the truth. Preach the doctrine of clean water and common sense. That is what the world needs; and the missionary who carries that creed into the homes of ignorance and of poverty will come in at the harvest bringing his sheaves with him."

Across the face of the exhorter flitted an expression half pity, half reproach; the next moment he sighed heavily; he had learned the folly of all argument with this man. He lifted his long arm that had aye been ready to do battle in the cause of his espousing, and said, in his best pulpit style:

"Let the dead bury their dead; the Master has sent me to *you*."

"No, sir, I reckon not," said the doctor, with something like a return to good humour. "You misunderstood the call, that was all. It was your common sense indicating a place where the cheer was plenteous, and a welcome possible. Well, you *are* welcome; make yourself at home while I speak to Aunt Dilcy. You know where the guest-chamber is."

He nodded towards the garret, and went to Aunt Dilcy, busy "taking up the breakfast."

She had just taken the pot of steaming coffee from' the stove, and at the moment he entered the kitchen was carefully dusting away with her apron any possible soot that might adhere to the bottom of the vessel. When he spoke she started, being unaware of his presence, and set the pot back upon the stove, with a vehemence that almost sent it spinning across the floor.

"Lor, marster," she exclaimed, "you mos' skeered de life out'n me; it's de befo' God's truf, you sholy s'prised me *some*."

"Well, I am going to surprise you still more," said the doctor. "The young man over at the miller's is dead."

"Great God A'mighty—"

"And you are to get your breakfast on the table and go over there. You are to carry this bill to Lissy. The miller has had losses lately, and something may be needed beyond their present funds. Give the money to Lissy herself, and tell her to use it as she may find need for it, and that she can repay it in eggs and butter sometime. Be sure you tell her that, else she will not touch it. And before you go, send Ephraim to take Brother Barry's mare."

Despite his rather stormy welcome, Brother Barry continued to occupy the guest-chamber for some weeks. With all his ignorance, the mountaineer was not ignorant of men; he knew that he was welcome, that his entertainment was given freely, without grudging; he knew, also, that in none of the humble valley homes within his charge would he find himself so comfortable, so free to come and go, so unquestionably at home. So he remained, and although the revival at Goshen furnished food for gossip as well as pleasure for the entire neighbourhood of believers, and although Brother Barry never for an instant failed to let his light shine in the eyes of the infidel, and never let slip an opportunity to speak a word of warning, still the doctor continued to "travel the high road to destruction," as the minister declared he was doing.

Many had been gathered into the fold, however, and among them Lissy, poor, pale, heart-broken Lissy Reams. Sorrow had so crushed her that Brother Barry found it no difficult task to persuade her that the Lord had visited her with the rod of His wrath. The doctor saw but little of her those days. There come to all of us points where life makes a certain, emphatic turn, after which all life is different, and runs, or seems to, in a new groove. Such a point had come to Alicia, and the shadow of her grief drew her into herself, away from those who would have offered comfort. He would have gone to her, only that he dared not. His impulse would have been to fold her in his arms and soothe her in his bosom, his own forever.

At last the meeting closed, and one morning in December the parson mounted his mare and rode out of the valley, back to the heights.

But even the hard shell of ignorance

had been pierced by the quiet goodness of the infidel. True, he had writhed not a little under his host's keen sarcasm and keener questioning; and there were times when he would have been glad to question him on certain points, but he was afraid, lest, showing his weak part to the enemy, he should be attacked in that quarter, overthrown perhaps, and conquered. Moreover, he believed in faith, accepting without questioning the gospel and its teaching. He was afraid to tamper with his religion lest he unsettle its foundation. Yet, in a certain way, he had a great respect for the doctor. As he sat astride his mare at parting, he leaned forward and placed a hand upon his shoulder.

"My brother," said he, "you have sat beneath the word day after day, hearing without heeding the gospel call. You are not a bad man. Neither are you a Christian. But you are in darkness: I want to help you to the light, to lead you to the Rock. Show me where you stand; tell me your creed. You believe in the hereafter? in God?"

The physician sighed. There was a time when the words would have amused him; but of late he had looked too steadily upon the sombre in life.

"I believe in God," he said, "yes; and in a hereafter, yes; for I am not a fool, though certainly not orthodox. Your theory of three Gods comprising one, no. Your God of vengeance, cruelty, and blood I refuse to accept. Jesus Christ preached the real religion. The creed which I profess is the same that He taught: truth, cleanliness, charity. My religion is told in few words: to tell the truth, help the poor, and keep myself clean."

The Methodist straightened himself to speak, but paused, reconsidered, and was silent a moment, looking away towards the hills where the mists were shrouded about Sewanee. There was a baffled expression in his eyes. He had toiled all these weeks for a certain fish, and at last had been forced to quit with an empty net. He lifted his hand towards the purple haze.

"Rain," said he. "Rain followed by drought, poor crops, sickness, destitution. I know the signs. Well, for me, I aim to trust in the Lord for a crop. I'll trust in the Lord."

"And keep the plough handy," laughed the doctor. "Don't forget to mix the plough in with your prayers, Brother Barry."

The shaft went home; there was a frown upon the face of the preacher as he rode across the valley; he felt the hot blood mount to his cheeks, recalling as he did the waste which last year Joe Bowen had converted into a garden, but which this spring, for lack of a friendly hand, was only an acre of weeds. He had been insulted,—he, a minister of the gospel. His wrath refused to be bridled. Suddenly he clinched his fist, half turned in the saddle, and exclaimed:

"That man's the dad-burndedest infidel this side o' hell, I reckin." It was the nearest he had ever been to swearing.

But later, when his anger had cooled, and his way lay along the cliffs, where the mists were lifted and the view clearer, and the blue heaven beamed upon him fair and open, the words of the infidel came back to him, and underneath their lightness he read a deeper meaning.

"To help the poor, and to keep myself clean."

He gave the lines a sudden jerk, and, as the mare came to a halt, thrust his hand into his coat pocket, where he carried a small, well-thumbed Bible, for the churches of his circuit were not always supplied with Bibles. Slowly he turned the leaves, until he found that which he sought, then read slowly, aloud, running his finger along the lines, while the mare with considerable forethought cropped the long dry grasses along the roadside.

"'*Pure religion and undefiled before God and the Father is this: to visit the fatherless and widows in their affliction, and to keep himself unspotted from the world.*'"

After all, the old doctor's creed was not unlike the definition given by the apostle; and that he lived up to it no man could deny.

He closed the book, replaced it in his bosom, gathered up his lines and rode on. There was nothing he could say against a creed so endorsed; and, after all, there might be that, in the books of which he knew nothing, which would give new light. But he was resolved to "cling to the safe side." The books might confound him. Too much learning might prove as dangerous as too little.

"I'd rather go it blind," he declared, "go by faith, and keep on the safe side." There entered into his brain no thought of a spiritual law which refuses to condone wilful blindness.

He chose to hug to his heart the old

doubtful comfort of "God, He did it." Chose to thus frighten ignorance, and lay the lash to the shoulders of weakness. Chose to believe in God's wrath, setting aside Christ's love. Alas! that man should so malign his Maker.

Chapter XII

THE day following Brother Barry's departure, the doctor left his servants in charge and went back to the city.

Winter passed, spring and summer drifted, and still he lingered. At last the snow came again; silence settled upon the valley, and brooded upon the finer heights of the more distant hills. With the first fall of snow he returned; fires were kindled, the blue smoke curled above the little hut, buried under its white burden; lights twinkled in the windows again, lighting the path through the valley and sending a good glow out upon the darkness for the cheer of belated travellers. For three days Doctor Boring remained indoors, seeing no one, adjusting himself anew to the life which had been temporarily broken into. And then, the fourth morning after his return, Lissy called.

He heard her voice in the hall, speaking first to Aunt Dilce and then to Zip.

He started, and turned cold; he had dreaded, longed, and steeled himself for this visit. Yet the sound of her voice, with its gentle, music-like cadences, started all his nerves a-jingling. It struck him that there was something new in the tones, something he had not heard there before; its presence cut him to the soul. His trained ear had detected in the first word she spoke the note of sorrow, keen, incurable, hopeless. Those who have suffered recognise the note in any sphere or circumstance.

He had not seen her since the day they buried Al. He had kept aloof purposely; he could bear her happiness, her content with her lover, but not her grief; he would undoubtedly have made her sorrow his. He had conquered himself before she entered, though his hand still shook, and there was a mist before his eyes when she opened the door and stood before him.

At the sight of her he forgot himself as utterly as though he had never felt a pang because of her. He felt nothing but her sorrow; saw nothing but her poor, pinched little face, with the purple shadows under the fathomless eyes that gazed into his with unspoken pain.

She was as frail as one of the lilies that had bloomed in his yard all autumn; and like the lily, she had been chilled by the frost that fell too early upon the shivering white petals.

He would scarcely have recognised her but for the golden hair knotted about the small, dainty head still crowned with the old red felt. Her very voice was changed; for sorrow makes for itself an abiding-place in the human voice. Otherwise she was the same gentle, quiet Alicia.

"Doctor Borin'," she said, extending her hand to meet his, "I'm mighty glad you have come back home again; I have missed you mightily."

There was a quiver in the voice, in spite of the powerful effort to hold it firm. A moisture gathered in the large, deep eyes, and a little hacking cough followed her attempt at welcome. Without a word he took her arm and led her to the fire, and stood scanning carefully the delicate, changed features. He was the physician again, and she the patient; that was all.

"Why, child, what have you done to yourself? Where is all your colour and where your strength? Why didn't you write me you were ill? Didn't you know I would have come to you, Lissy? that the whole world couldn't have —"

He remembered, and stopped; but the tone of his voice caught her ear. She was weak and overwrought and nervous. His words and tone quite overcame her poor strength. She clasped her poor trembling hands and burst into tears.

Resisting the impulse to take her to his heart, he drew up his own easy chair, tucked her into it, and said:

"You are not fit to be out in weather like this. Now you are to sit there and thaw out, and after awhile I am going to give you a tonic. Now then, throw off your hat. You are to spend the day, and knock Zip off or he will be in your lap. And now tell me about it. How long have you been ill?"

He drew up a chair and seated himself beside her, watching with the physician's practised eye the come and go of colour in the delicate cheeks, the play of breath in the rise and fall of the chest, the nervous tears ready to start at a word.

"I haven't been sick, Doctor Borin'," she said. "I fetched you the fresh aigs I've been waiting to fetch you, to pay up my debts to you. Aunt Dilce wouldn't take any while you ware gone, because she said you didn't tell her, an' the hens on the place laid enough for her and Ephraim. But I reckin I can begin again now; I'd like to pay my debt. You ware mighty good to remember me that time,—an' to send the money. I don't know what I'd 'a' done but for you. You air mighty good anyhow, mighty good to me."

He saw that she was unnerved, ready to break down; it required all his strength not to break down himself and pour out the burden of his love. Once he did put out his hand for the little pale one lying upon Zip's shaggy head that rested against her knee; but he remembered in time to lay his fingers upon the wrist instead, where the pulse was throbbing nervously in the small blue veins.

"I'd like to do somethin' for you-uns, Doctor Borin'," Alicia went on, in her low, musical voice. "I useter think you ware not happy over here by yourse'f, an'

I wish I could do somethin' to make you more happy —"

The hand upon her wrist trembled. Did she know what she was saying? Did she mean that which her words implied? If so, would his unspoken promise to Joe hold? Did she understand the situation, and was she trying to help him out of his difficulty?

"I'd like to wash yo' clothes even, or he'p Aunt Dilce when I get better; I feel that obligated to you."

He dropped her arm and, leaning back in his chair, said, quietly:

"We will talk about that when you are strong again. Now, Lissy, will you answer my question? How long have you been ill?"

"I haven't been sick, Doctor Borin'; I got overhet at the meetin' last spring, and took a cold. Seems to 'a' settled somewheres, and not minded to let go."

"Settled hell!—" he exclaimed, and

then stopped. A shadow, deeper than that which had made its home there, came into the large eyes. She lifted her hand to check the wicked exclamation at which, in other days, she had been wont to laugh so merrily.

"I wish you wouldn't," she said; "you air so good, it air a pity to spoil it with such words. I wish you wouldn't. If not for your own sake, then just to pleasure me."

Was there anything he would not have done "to pleasure" her?

"I'll quit," he replied, "to please *you*. But I was about to say something warm. Instead I shall give you something warm for that cough. Suppose I whip up an egg-nog with one of your own eggs; then we shall see if you are putting off bad eggs upon your old customers; see?"

She did not respond to his joking; her face wore a troubled look.

"I'd rather you wouldn't," she said. "It's made of liquor, egg-nog air, an' it's wrong to drink liquor. I'd rather cough as to do wrong."

Her conversion had been complete,— its completeness baffled him.

"Well, then," he replied, "here is a cough mixture that I keep for just such obstinate cases as yours; we will try this."

He poured some of the dark liquid into a tumbler and watched her drink it, wondering the while at the change her new religion had wrought. On a former visit she had drunk a glass of wine, and had carried that which remained in the bottle to Al, declaring it would "do him a sight of good if he enjoyed the taste of it as well as she did." How she had changed, her very voice and speech; she had adopted the slow, drawling dialect of her grandparents, as though in adopting their creeds she must shoulder their ignorance and lack of culture also.

The tonic revived her; he saw the

glow spring to eye and cheek, and he felt better for its presence, though he recognised it as only a delusion, a false reflection of health, produced by the stimulating medicine.

She folded her hands upon her lap and watched him shyly from under her long, dark lashes; but it was many minutes before she could bring herself to the point of giving him her entire confidence. After awhile her fingers began to work nervously, pulling at the fringe of her gay plaid shawl. He felt that she was bracing herself for an ordeal.

"I have come to see you," she said, at last, "about — about somethin'."

"Oh, you have, have you?" he said, with an effort at careless humour.

"Doctor Borin'," she began, in her quaint drawl, "they calls you-uns an infidel."

"Yes," said the doctor, "that is no news, Lissy. I have heard that often; ever since I came to the valley, and for more than twenty years before," he added. "They are welcome to call me what they choose; it is not what others think us, but that which we know ourselves to be, should trouble or please us in this life."

"But," said Alicia, ignoring the interruption, "they allow that you know right smart, too. Gran'father says he'd about as lief take your say-so as to take Brother Barry's. He says Brother Barry ware never fifty mile from Pelham in all his born days, an' don't know if the word be preached in Tennessee like it be in Georgy, not to save his life. He says one man has as much right to his say as another man, an' to his belief, too. But granny, she says hell's a-bilin' with unbelievers like you-uns, though even she admits you are entitled to a hearin' at the last day, *if* the infidel gets his entitlements."

"Oh, I'll get mine, Lissy," said the doctor. "Don't you fret about that. I will get a hearing, if God is good. You believe He is good, do you not, Lissy?"

The slender hands were clasped with sudden rhapsody, a light leaped to the quiet, fathomless eyes, there was rapture in the face, — the rapture, the light, and the excitement of the fanatic. The physician saw it and understood; his heart dropped like lead in his bosom. Too late, too late; the deed had been done. He felt as he had sometimes felt when summoned to attend a wounded man, and, arriving too late, had found the man dead. The heart had ceased beating, a little piece of anatomical mechanism had stopped, that was all. Yet it meant that somebody had committed a murder.

"Oh, He air," said Alicia, softly, and with strange fervour, "He air good! God air good! I give my testimony to hit. He air good — good; Doctor Borin', I have found peace since I ware here aforetimes."

His heart beat so fiercely he could

scarcely trust himself to speak, to talk to her, his poor broken flower. They had played upon her heart in its desolation; taken advantage of her sorrow, her ignorance, her loneliness, and her need of sympathy. He understood all in an instant, and wondered where Joe could have been, and what doing, that he had failed to fit himself to the emptiness left by the beloved brother. Peace, indeed! He leaned forward, took the slender, tear-wet hands in his own, folded them gently between his strong, warm palms. Thus would he have folded her life in his, warmed and caressed the quivering, wounded heart. But such was not reserved for him; he might minister as the physician, the friend, the old man versed in the knowledge of books,—no more.

"My child," he said, "you have found peace, you tell me; yet your face, your restlessness, your very voice, all tell me you have *not* found peace; that you are far from it. What is it, Alicia? What is the trouble? Peace that comes of God is His blessed gift, and 'He addeth no sorrow thereto.' Tell me what troubles you, my child, and let me help you, just as your father would. I am an old man, but not insensible to human pain. Some hearts refuse age in spite of tottering old bodies and heads that catch the snowfall. Mine is young enough to take your grief and help you to a way out of it, maybe; but if it be one of those burdens — they fall sometimes — which must be borne, I am ready to help you lift it, bear it —" Share it, he was about to say. His heart yearned to take her into its protecting warmth, to bless her poor life with the fullness of his love.

The gentle tone and touch brought the tears against which she had been struggling.

"I want to do right. But it's hard, hard, hard. I want to ask you, Doctor Borin', is it wrong to marry a man who ain't a believer? Is it a sin to?"

Poor little ignorant! the great trouble had been laid bare at last.

"It's Joe," she continued. "You said I ought — to marry Joe. You told me so, and I meant to, because you said it was only fair to him. But since then I've got religion. Joe's a sinner; I don't know as I could make him happy; an' I didn't want to marry — only you said 'twas right. But Brother Barry he allows God will lay it up against me if I marry Joe; 'punish me,' he called it. Like He punished me befo' when He took little Al. He says that's what made Al die. God was angry with me fur bein' a sinner; an' He couldn't fetch me to a sense o' sin no other way, an' so He took my brother. My poor little brother Al! Seems to me He might 'a' got me some other way, an' not have took my brother. But Brother Barry says God's ways is past findin' out, an' I reckin they air. But I can't see my way clear to do *anything*; 'pears to me I'm left alone, now Al's gone; an' Joe's always been good to me, an' I ain't got anybody else, Doctor Borin', nobody; an' I have asked for light, for help; an' it has — not — come."

What could he say? what do? To him the thing that was so simple, so easy to adjust and to set right, was to her a tragedy.

To tell her she was a child, an innocent, and that Brother Barry was a fool or a fanatic, would have been a useless waste of words. Six months earlier, Alicia, the "sinner," would have laughed at the prophecy of the preacher, and made merry over his threats. But Alicia, the convert, her heart sore with the desolation of death, was ready to hug to itself any promise of consolation, and to flee any threat of a second visitation of sorrow.

He felt as helpless as she. For the cancerous teachings of ignorance there is no healing save in knowledge; and the mind diseased, unlike the body, will not bear the knife at the root of the woe; it requires gentle handling, time, and the tender tricks of art to woo it back to health. Hers was a present need; she being one of those all-soul creations, whose fires, once lighted, will turn upon and consume itself in its own flame. He forbore severe treatment. To her, although she still respected his great knowledge and admired his undeniable goodness, he was still an infidel, a non-partaker in the feast of the saints. His heart was as sore as hers; still he must say something, since she had come to him for help.

"Alicia," he began, " Brother Barry has presented to you but one view of the great God; there is another, child —"

She silenced him with her hand. "Oh, I have been a sinner, I have been a sinner, Doctor Borin'; God might burn me in the lake of fire and still be too good to me. I know it, I know it."

He sighed, discouraged at the outset. But there was another string upon which he might sound for a response.

"Alicia," he said, "you are considering only yourself in this matter. Listen to me. When God puts into the heart of an honest, earnest man, as you believe God does, a love for an earnest, tender woman, He puts the feeling there to bless and enrich both his life and hers. Such love may not be lightly set aside. There are consequences, fearful and destructive, which sometimes do and always may attend cruelty to one who loves us. I know whereof I speak."

She was silent, knowing that he referred to his own unhappy experience. After a moment he continued: "You have no right to spoil Joe's happiness for a whim. No true woman will grieve the heart that loves her."

Still she made no reply; she was afraid of him, afraid to trust him, afraid to trust herself. Above all, she was afraid of her religion; it had become her tyrant; she was ready to sacrifice whatever it might demand; not only her love, but her life as well.

"Alicia," he said, studying carefully the varying shadows of her face, "is this your only reason for refusing Joe?"

She started, flushed, and, without replying, rose to go. He also rose, and, scarcely knowing that he did so, put himself between the door and her.

"You must answer my question; tell me, before I let you go, if religious motives alone influence you in your refusal to become the wife of Joe Bowen."

There was a flash of the gray eyes, a curl of the thin, bloodless lip. She lifted her hand, as of one about to take an oath. Instead, however, she waved him out of her path.

"Stand out of my way," she commanded. "I am obligated to no man so much that I must take oath to every foolish thought I ever had, as I can *see*."

He laughed and moved aside to let her pass. Her simple effort at parrying, her refusal to deny the suggestion carried in his questioning, her excitement that was embarrassment more than anger,—all these spoke more than her simple admission could have spoken, and he was content.

It is enough sometimes to know oneself beloved, without the additional joy of possession.

He stood a moment at the little gate through which she had passed, to watch her climbing the brown path, winding in and out the denuded, snow-rimmed mountain growth. Her dress of blue homespun, the large-plaided, many-hued shawl, the bright head wearing its crown of gay felt,—all these combined to make a rare dash of colour against the dead whiteness of the landscape.

Three times she paused to rest, while only the preceding summer she had come down that same path with the light step of a mountain doe, and cheeks to shame the roses that had bloomed beside her door. Alas, the roses were all dead, alike in garden and young life.

"And all so unnecessary," said the doctor, still watching the bright confusion of colour disappearing among the grayness of the heights. She would not climb beyond the clouds, poor Alicia; she would only pass into the gloom of the confusing mists. He sighed, and turned back to his cabin. "She will be dead before another winter. I might have saved her once, and both of us been happy. But not now, not now. Fanaticism is stronger than affection; hers, with Al's death to help along, will soon end it all for her,— my poor Alicia."

It came sooner than he expected. All spring he watched her fade. The roses came again to the bush by the cabin door, but not to the cheek of the fading girl. She came and went as usual, still brought her offering of fresh eggs and butter, though now she left them with old Dilce in the kitchen. Her chats with the doctor were limited to short resting spells at the gate, where he sometimes hailed her on her trips to and from Sewanee. These meetings were as much a torture to him as they were to her; she was not in his life now, nor of it; his own hand had put her from him. If he could have heard from her own lips, just once before she went from him, a tender word, could have had one assurance that the pure young heart was his, he could have felt that to lay her in her grave was sweeter than to yield her to another. But, try as he might, he could never surprise her into a betrayal of affection, if indeed she harboured any for him. Only once — it was the last visit she made to him — he had thought to probe her heart by an unexpected reference to Joe. She had almost fallen into the snare he had set.

"You owe it to him," he declared, "to marry him. He is going to the dogs. I saw him drunk last week."

She recoiled and cried out so sharply he winced for the hurt he had dealt her.

"I can't," she sobbed. "Oh, I can't;

I want to do what seems to me right to do, but I can't — marry — nobody."

One June morning, when the winds sang low in the forest, they sent for him. The miller met him at the gate and bade him go in.

"She'll soon be at rest, poor Lissy," he said, "an' free o' all tormentin'. She ware a likely gal, an' a happy one, befo' trouble tuk holt of her. Trouble come to her, an' they were not satisfied, but they must pile worry 'pon top of hit till she sunk under it. Go in, Doctor Borin', an' help my little gal ter die."

Granny stood in the doorway, awed and tearless, a strange subdued sorrow in her face. She moved aside to let him pass, pointing with her long finger to the little room where the honeysuckle peeped in at the window and the June winds stole through the curtains of simple muslin to fan the brow of the sick girl. Granny had long ago recognised the fact that

Lissy had passed beyond the skill of either infidel or herb.

Alicia was awake, restless and tossing, a wild light in her eyes and a strange strength in the worn body.

The physician stepped to the bedside and spoke her name softly: "Alicia?"

At the sound of his voice she lifted herself in bed and cried out to him, sharply:

"Doctor Borin', oh, Doctor Borin', don't let me die." She caught his coat front and held it as he bent over her, seeking to soothe and reassure her, although his heart was breaking with her piteous pleadings for life.

"I'm afeard, oh, I'm afeard to die. I'm afeard the devil will get me. Do you reckin the devil will get me, Doctor Borin'? I've been a-thinkin' about what you said, an' I'm afeard I done wrong after all, treatin' of Joe so bad. But I meant it fur right. Oh, I did try to do right; I did, I did, I did."

It was too cruel, after all her struggle and sacrifice, to be so harassed at the last!

He drew a chair to the bedside and folded the wasted, trembling hands in his.

"Oh, you poor child," he said. "Have you been worrying over my foolish scolding? You did right, of course, perfectly right; and you're not to give the matter another thought. I will tell Joe that you thought of him and were sorry that you hurt him, if you wish me to do so; and he will forgive you, Alicia; I am sure of it."

"Oh, I wish't you would," she sobbed. "Tell him I'm sorry I had — to hurt him. Air you sure he won't be mad at me?"

"Perfectly sure, Alicia. May I take him your love? Must I tell him that you knew that you loved him — *at the last?*"

He bent his face to hers; he saw the old hurt, haunted expression return to her eyes. But she smiled, even in the face of death; the principle that had sealed her lips against the comforting lie spoke a comforting, a blessed truth to him.

"You do not love him, Alicia? Is that it? You love another? One who held you in heart from the first moment he saw you, dear? You loved him a little in return, for all he was so old, so much too old for you, my poor darling?"

She nestled closer to him; her fingers closed upon his with convulsive strength.

"Don't tell him," she begged. "Don't ever let Joe know; it wouldn't do any good — now."

"It is enough that I know, dear," he said, with broken voice. "I shall take him your love, your dear love, the same you might have sent to Al. May I?"

She nodded, and was silent. The shadowy eyes held many a doubt in their startled depths.

"Rest easy now," said the doctor,

"and be happy. You have been a good girl, and have tried to do your duty."

He stooped and touched her forehead with his lips lightly, as one caresses a rose, afraid of bruising the tender petals. He pushed the golden strands of hair back from the brow that death had kissed, and saw her smile, as though the unutterable sweetness of the caress were the one touch of earth, being so like divine, she would carry with her to make paradise more perfect.

Only a moment, one poor little moment of bliss, and the old horror, the fear of that which might await her when she should pass into the far mysterious, returned to torture her.

"Don't let me die." The poor plaintive pleading hurt his very soul to hear.

"I'm afeard to go down into the pit, Doctor Borin'! I'm afeard of — God."

"Afraid of the good God, dear? Think of Him, Alicia. He alone can help you now. Remember only that He is the good God; good, good."

"An' the devil won't get me? Oh, I'm afeard of the devil, an' the fire that burns, an' never stops burnin'. Don't let me die an' go to the devil, Doctor Borin'!"

She was weeping wildly; her terror was pitiful. He knelt by the bed and took the fragile, wasted form in his arms, holding her closely, so that she lay upon his bosom like a frightened bird with broken wings fluttering helplessly. Granny came in and stood over the foot of the couch; grandad had gone to fetch a neighbour; old Dilce had come over to offer the assistance which she had learned was necessary at such times. The doctor neither saw nor heard anything but the dying girl in his arms. She was his for the moment; to him it had been granted to soothe the last moment of the life that had been so dear to him. He threw aside all disguise: he would speak the truth as he believed it, let the result be what it might.

"Lissy," he said, his face near her own, "listen to me, dear child. There is no devil. There is no devil and no lake of fire. Can you hear me, Lissy? And do you understand?"

Into the frightened eyes crept an expression of wonder that mellowed into perfect joy.

"Air you *sure?*" she whispered. "Sure he can't get me?"

"As I am that you are going straight to God, dear. Don't you be afraid; don't think of death at all; just remember the good God. You know Him, Lissy?"

She drew a long, deep sigh. "Oh, yes, I know *Him*. I'm so glad, so glad there ain't any devil. I was so afeard of him, and now there ain't any, there ain't any."

She nestled her head against his bosom; the heavy lids dropped wearily. Granny put her apron to her face and went out to nurse her grief alone. Old Dilce began to move the medicine bottles from the little candle-stand at the bed's side. She knew they would be needed no more.

But Doctor Boring neither stirred nor spoke, nor moved his eyes from the beautiful face upon his bosom. He was waiting for the last recognition, which he felt sure would not be denied him. There was a moment of intense silence before Alicia lifted her hand and placed it upon his bosom. He moved it gently to his neck, when she opened her eyes, shadowless now, and smiled. With the smile came a sigh, a breath of inexpressible content. The smile, the sigh, spoke to him, a wordless message, but he understood and was content. He put her back upon the pillow, wordless and without tears, and passed out where death had entered. His hand, as he passed, brushed a large full-hearted rose that bloomed upon the bush beside the door; the crimson petals fell apart and lay about his feet. It was well the rose should fade,—he wondered if it might not know that she was dead. The little tragedy in hearts was played. Henceforth life would wear its gray; return to its old silence. Into the heart's Holy of Holies only memory, the high priest, might enter.

The days multiplied to weeks, the weeks and months drifted drowsily into years, and autumn, purple with haze, and steeped with the odour of fading vegetation, was come again. The Indian pipes were in bloom, and where the goldenrod had died, bunches of gray stubble waved in the October wind.

In the doctor's cabin the fires had been lighted, for the nights were cool. He still went about among his sick, doing a quiet good. The guest-chamber sheltered but few now, since Brother Barry had been sent upon a different circuit. Sometimes Joe Bowen would lodge there, but not often; he had become restless after Alicia's death, and was fond of roaming the woods alone of nights, although he often came over to sit afternoons in the sunshine and talk with the doctor of Alicia. So changed, so softened, so gently patient was he, that Doctor Boring sometimes found it difficult to trace in the quiet, steady farmer the old fiery-tempered Joe who had once commanded him to come out and fight for the girl they both loved.

Only in one respect was he unchanged, — he was still proof against Brother Barry.

"I ain't got no religion, Doctor Borin'," he was wont to declare, "no more than I had when Lissy Reams useter name me for a sinner. An' I don't know no more than I did then. But, Doctor Borin'," — and his voice would fall to a low, not unmusical cadence, — "when they talk of Christ I seem to see Him wanderin' through the mount'n, lonesomin' an' weary, huntin' for the strays amongst His sheep.

An', oh! I feels for Him, I feels for Him. I know what 'tis to be a lonesome wanderer in the mount'ns. I know what 'tis to feel the rocks and thorns that cut an' prick. I know what 'tis to be forgot of all, except, maybe, of Him, who lived alone and lonesome, too; though I ain't unmindful of the word she sent ter me, her love an' her good-by. I remembers them, and they air sweet to me. But they air not that which comforts me; its *Him*, Him who suffered, too; an' so I say I feels for Him, Christ or elder brother, Son of God or son of man, which you will. He's nigh to me; His presence holps me. Somehows I don't look to reach the heights, where the skies air fair an' the eagles swim. But I'm content ter walk the valley path so long as *He* walks with me."

And with a sigh, half sad and half resigned, he lifts his eyes to the purpling hills where Alicia sleeps underneath the soughing hemlocks; where in summer the cows couch under the shadow of the cliffs, hard by Sewanee, and in winter the wind, like a spent runner, moans among the trees, lamenting, mayhap, those baffling mysteries, which to her have been at last made plain.

THE END.

www.ingramcontent.com/pod-product-compliance
Lightning Source LLC
Chambersburg PA
CBHW031349230426
43670CB00006B/485